MAMUTTY CHOLA

First published in 2018 by

Becomeshakespeare.com

Wordit Content Design & Editing Services Pvt Ltd
Unit - 26, Building A -1, Nr Wadala RTO,
Wadala (East), Mumbai 400037, India
T: +91 8080226699

Copyright © 2018, Mamutty Chola

All rights reserved. Any unauthorized reprint or use of this material is prohibited. No part of this book may be reproduced or transmitted in any form or by any means, electronic or mechanical, including photocopying, recording, or by any information storage and retrieval system without express written permission from the author/publisher.

Please do not participate in or encourage piracy of copyrighted materials in violation of the author's rights. Purchase only authorized editions.

©

ISBN - 978-93-88573-93-1

Dedication:

Dedicated to my wife SHABNAM, daughter ZEENAT, son AKBAR, grand son ETHAN and son-in law DWAYNE but for their love and support it would have been impossoble to give shape to MY inner feelings for fellow human beings.

ABOUT THE AUTHOR

Mamutty, Chola, Poet, in URDU AND ENGLISH, Writer, HR and Management Expert, WORKED AS General Manager HR with with International airports Authority of India, IPCL, HFC and SR VP CORPORATE HR with Ispat group.In Consultancy since 2000

Did schooling at Port Blair, Graduation from Madras, LLB from Agra University PGPM FROM Bombay and ADVANCED MANNAGEMENT COURSE FROM Templeton Management Institute, OXFORD, UK. He is recipient of UDYOG RATAN AWARD from Institute of Economics Studies, New Delhi for his contributions in the field of HR

INTRODUCTION:

Focus: Sharing my life experience of more than 45 years both as corporate hr, consultant and social activist. We all live for self but sharing the feelings of fellow humans is always enriching. I always believe in sharing. is growing.

The 300 plus poems cover all aspects of human life, nature and animals on mother earth. Hope the readers will find resonance of their lives in these poems. I believe sharing is growing.

INDES

My Father	18
Mother's Love	20
Prayers For My Daughter	21
My Little Angel-Ethan (My Grand Son)	22
How Long This Shadow Of Gloom	23
Blessed Are Those In Love	25
I Love Nature And Life	27
Loving Memories	29
I Love Sea Waves	31
Wine And Man	32
Souls Separated	34
Soul Is Supreme	35
Eyes Never Tell Lie	37
Love Is Care	38
Where Are You My Love?	40
Never Break The Trust	42
Be Fait hful To Your Partn er In Life	43
Mother Earth's Cry	44
What Is The Realit y Of Soul?	46
Loneliness Vs Solitude	47
Dreams Realization	49
Hope Creates Future	51
Magic Of Positive Thought	53
That Stanger	54
Our Musical Earth	56
Loneliness Of My Heart	58
Bondage Of Pain	60

Infinite Wait	61
Positive Thinkers Are Victors	62
Years Ago	63
Why Soul Is Sad Today	64
Appearances Are Always Diceptives, Mind You	65
Oh My Love	66
Our Country – India	67
My Lost Love	69
Broken Dreams	70
Pillow As Confidant	71
Gift Of Love	72
Grip Of Sadness	74
March Of Human Civilzation	75
Those Memorable Days	76
Me And Sea Waves	82
Memory And Loneliness-Relation	84
Love Is Bliss	85
Love And Hate	86
Tender Heart	87
I Love Life	88
Live Life Like Seasons	90
Feelings And Emotions	91
Happiness Is Hidd en In Your Thoughts	92
Still Wait For Thy Welfare	93
Who Has Seen Tomorrow?	94
World Without Love Is A Tomb	95
Bondage Of Life	97
The Abyss In My Life	99
Season Comes Back But Not Gone Time	100
I Love Darkness	102
The Life	103
Song Of Your Memory	104

Not Destined To Be Mine	105
Heart Vs Mind	106
Pains Of Separtion	107
Change Or Revenge?	108
You Are Always Within Me	110
Beauty Of Death Is Matcless	111
Pang Of Separation	112
Always Live In Today	113
Love Is Supreme	115
Our First Meeting	116
Lessons From Death	118
Love Is Life	119
Meadows Of Bliss	120
Can Love Be The Currency Of The World ?	121
Never Live Life With Expectation	122
Beauty Of Human Heart	123
Beauty Of Eyes	124
Bilissful Soul	125
Love Is God	126
Tears In Rain	127
Tongue Is Tender But Few Can Handle	129
Success Is A Journey	130
For Years	131
Treat Your Wine As Your Beloved	132
Buds Go Wither	133
Truth Is Always Lonely	134
Tears Are Language Of Silence	135
Emeregence Of India Of Ours	136
Music Is The Language Of Soul	138
Made For Each Other	140
Smile Is Powerful Than Words	141
Love -The Essence Of Life	143

Our Lives Are Transient Like Sparks	144
Beauty Lies Within Us	145
Uderstand True Love	146
Poetry, Nature's Language	147
Silence 'S Song Is Voiceless	148
What Is Beauty	150
That Innocent Look	151
Immortal Bond With Beloved	152
Promis es Like Floatin g Clouds	153
Who Cares?	154
Smile A Free Investment In Goodwill	155
My Heart Is Restless Today	156
Came Like A Fairy	158
You Are My Love,My Love	159
My Destiny	160
Friendship In Love	162
It Been Years Since We Parted	163
What Is Your Relations With?	164
Gifts Of Nature	165
When I Sit Back And Reflect—	166
Separated Never Meet	167
You Are My Love	169
Magic Of Self Admiration	170
Me And My Memories	172
My Journey Of Loneliness	173
Lesson Of Loyalty	174
Lesson From Death	176
Oh! My Life	177
Autumn Amidst Spring	178
Never Wait For Gone Time	179
Songs Of Memory	180
Your Are Matchless, My Love	181

On Time Canvas	182
There was a time	183
In Praise Of Moon	184
Within Small Acts Of Love —	185
Poetry Of Earth Is Infinite	187
If Love Is Religion, World Is Paradise	188
All Creatures Are Created In Pairs	189
Every Night Has A Dawn	190
Beloved's Wait For Her Love	191
Magic Of Love	192
Why Are You Sad At Heart?	194
Chanced Meeting With My Lost Love	195
Oh My Darling Love	197
Listen To The Cry Of Your Feelings	198
Rain Makes Me Nostalgic	199
Love The Life	200
My Concerns For Loved Ones	201
Secret Of Happiness	202
Flight Of Imaginati on	204
Solitude Of My Heart	205
Oh My Betrayed Love	206
Why Are You Sad? Oh Moon Why	207
In Conversation With My Soul	209
Listen To Mind Not Heart	210
Love Is Immortal	212
Helplesness	214
Together With My Love	215
Say Good Bye	216
All Are Selfish To The Core	217
Love Is God	218
In Separation Loves Flourishes	219
Paradox Of Human Relationship	220

Feelings And Emotions	221
Life Is Celebrations	222
The Widening Divide In Society	223
My Long Cherished Hope	224
Message Of Life	226
Acts Of Kindness	228
Consicience Dies In Silence	229
March Of Humanity	230
Peace Is Omnipotent	231
Changing Relationships	232
Tender Heart	234
Causes Of Destruction	235
Think High Always	236
Who Am I?	238
My Little Doll -Zeenat	240
We All Are One	241
Life Is Gift Of Creator	242
Be A Creator Of One's Destiny	243
Life Means Sharing	245
Realities Of Life	247
Liberated Slaves!	248
Keep Your Thought Right	250
As You Sow So You Reap	251
Be A Gardener In Life	253
Have Feelings For Nature	254
Mumbai's Localtrain	255
Slums Of Mumbai	257
Mumbai's Juhu Beach	258
From Dust You Came To Dust You Go	260
Trust Once Broken, Broken For Ever	261
Bitter Truth	262
Life Is Transient	263

Never Lose Your Individuality	265
War For Peace	266
Two Faced World	267
Emerging Dreams	268
Never Be Slave Of Your Ego	270
This Wonderful World Of Ours	271
Leaders; Traders In Dreams	272
Never Trade In People's Faith	274
Your Work Should Speak	275
There Are World Beyond Stars	276
Wonder Of Youth	277
Do Not Fool Innocents	278
Who Has Time For You?	280
Knowledge Speaks, Wisdom Listens	281
Mirror And Shade Best Friends	282
Conscience Is Chamber Of Justice	283
Voice Of Reason	284
No One Is Perfect In The World	285
Never Been Good War Or Bad Peace	286
Breaking News Of 21 St Century	287
No Time For Self	288
Wonder Of Human Mind	289
To Sink You Need To Be Alive	290
War Means Destruction, Not Peace	291
Happiness Reason For Beauty	292
Ignorance Is Bliss	293
Ho God You Are Merciful	294
Success Is A Journey	295
Curse Of Hate	296
Relationship Is Like Gardening	298
Truth Is Always Lonely	299
Lif e Is A Good Teacher	300

Tears Are Language Of Silence	301
Criteria Of Success	302
Dogs Are Best Friends	304
Inspiration From Lion	306
Theist, Atheist And Agnostic	307
Made For Each Other	309
Live Life With A Mission	310
Fight For Equality Is Against Nature	311
Our Lives Are Transient Like Sparks	313
Change And Self Interest Only Permanent	314
Homo Sapiens Are Dominant	315
Nature's Benevolence	316
Never Change Your Values	318
Equality Is Impossible	320
What Is Hope?	321
No Success Is Infinite	322
True Religion Is Humanism	323
Equality Vs Equal Opp ortunity	324
Past Is A Dead Yesterday	325
Genius Has Limitation, Stupidity None!!	326
Mystery Thy Name Is Woman	327
Words Of Wisdom	328
Genius Is A Superman In A Man	330
Realities Of Life	332
Life Is A Gift Of Nature	334
Do Change Your Opinion, Never Value	335
Men's Stupidity Is Infinite	336
Silence Is God	337
Trust Is Two Way Traffic	338
Revenge Is A Two-Edged Sword	339
Human Civilization	340
Self Interest Supreme	341

Power Of Courage Is Infinite	343
Enthusiasm Key To Success	344
Real Freedom	345
Miracle Of Struggle	346
Compromise Is The Name Of The Marriage	347
Setback Is An Event Not Deaeat	348
Power Of Ideas	349
Power Of Sacrifice	350
One Who Is Afraid Will Tell Lie	351
Change Is Life	352
Magic Of Positive Thought	353
Every One Deserves	354
Power Of Integrity	355
Magic Of Failures	356
Failure Build s Character	357
Jealousy Is Blind	358
Departed Never Comes Back	359
Fame Is Transient	361
Life Is A Suspense	362
The Change Is Permanent	363
Faith In God	364
May Asifa Soul Rest In Peace	365
Underst and Life	366
A Man With Courage Is Majority	367
Bigger The Problem Greater Is The Success.	368
Genius Is A Superman In A Man	369
Let Us Save Mother Earth	372
Trust Is Life	374
God Is Omnipresent	375
Thrills Of Childhood	377
Nature's Miracle	378
Trust Is Foudation Of Human Society	380

Truth Is All Power	381
Time Is Omnipotent	382
First Deserve	383
Death Is Certain	384
Reflections	385
Evlution Of Human Society	386
Message Of Wisdom	388
Every Day Is Gift Of God	389
Journey of Excellence	390
Fall From Faultless To Fault	391
Dynamics Of Thoughts And Actions	392
Life Is A Sojourn On Earth	394
An Utopian Dream	396
Time And Circumstances	398
Power Of Imagination	399
Nature Believes In Change	401
Live Like Mirror	403
Voice Of Sanity	405
I Am Time	406
Aim For Better World	409
All Fame Transient	410
Deserving Gets Rewards, Needy Charity	412
Relation Between Thought And Action	413
Have A Look Around	414
Strange Are Ways Of Human Thinking	416
Reap As You Sow	417
Don't Be A Prisoner Of Loneliness	418
Tough Time Never Lasts	419
Food For Thoughts	421
My Homage To Our Beloved Atalji	423
Does God Listen To All?	424
What Is Faith?	425

Secrets Of Happiness	426
Magic Of Language Is Infinite	427
Genesis Of Culture Is In Smile	429
Life Means Struggles	431
Journey Of Life	432
Man And Nature	433
Simplicty, Tolerance And Kindness	434
What Is Disappointment?	435
Death Is Certain Why To Fear	436
Right Thinking	437
Journey Of Honesty Is Always Lonely,	439
Why To Act As Blind?	441
Mirror Does Not Reflects Truth All The Time	443
Voice Of Reason	444
Busyness And Loneliness	445
Curse Of Poverty	447
Withering Relationships	449
Promise Of Togetherness	451
Our Tomorrow Is Hidden In Today!!!	452
My Native Place Andaman And Nicobar Islands	453
Music Is Language Of Nature	455
Mirror's Submission	456
Circumstances Reasons For Worries	457
Time Is Invicible	458
Tribute To Father Of The Nation	459
My Love, My Partner In Life	460
Friends And Foes	462
Saga Of Moter's Glory	463
True Love Is Immortal	465
Success Is A Transit Camp	466

My Father

I was a little boy when father passed away
I have treasured his memory deep down in my heart

He would say share happiness with all
Lead life like candle or "Deep"

You can light thousand candles
with one candle without losing your light

I still remember his glowing face
He would decorate our house
With candles during Diwali

His religion was humanism
His heritage made me a tolerant human being

His advice to us would be God lives within us
Neither in Kaaba, nor temple or church either

My poetry have sparks of, his values
Which I now share with fellow humans

My pen name Deep Andamani is not a coincident
This is a gift of my father's heritage to me

Like candle I live to spread message of love
Love unites, removes hatred and brings smiles,

Hatred and intolerance only divide and
Bring destruction all around, life is too short FOR HATE.

By Mamutty chola

MOTHER'S LOVE

Lucky are those who are blessed with mothers's love
Mother is symbol of love, and sacrifice.

Mother love is like an **eternal** light and infinite
Deeper than the ocean, as exalted as sky, as bright as galaxy of stars.

Mother's love echoes in the entire universe.
Mother is called --MA; be it china, India, USA,
UK, Russia, Persia. Iran or Iraq.

Mother's prayers and love help one to conquer the world.
In all religions, mother's place is supreme

Those unfortunates, who are deprived of mother's love,
carry within them an emptiness devoid of love till their death;

The vacuum being unfathomable such persons lives remain
incomplete. In the changing world I am witness to the tragic cases

where mothers are left all alone uncared and unattended
in the old age by their loved ones. A direct reflection of changing
values in the society.

Such people suffer the worst in this world itself.
Mother's love is the only love which is selfless

And there is no substitute to mother love.
For that reason only; Quran says paradise is at mother's feet,

By Mamutty chola

PRAYERS FOR MY DAUGHTER

Be your heart free from hatred
Be your life cradle of smile
Be your life ever free from anger
Be your life a symbol of peace
Be your life an abode of tranquillity
Be your life a source of joy always
Be you the reason for compassion
Be there no shadow of worry in your life
Be the journey of your life pleasant ever
Be you remain protected against all evils
Be your being always the refuge of love
Be you the darling of your loved ones
Be your life a role model for less fortunate
Be you like the morning breeze for loved ones
Be your life be evergreen like olive tree
Be you the centre of affections of all.
Be you blessed with success in all pursuits.

By Mamutty chola

My Little Angel-Ethan
(My Grand Son)

This little angel since he came to our lives
He has brought love, joy and bliss in our lives

He has filled our lives with smiles and smiles
Hidden in his smiles are message of love
Like a dawn of spring in our lives with morning breeze

His smiles have magical effect and vibrate with ecstasy
when calls us our souls dance with heavenly bliss

He gets angry with us as tantrum to agree to his innocent demands
When he comes and hug's us with love, no words to express our feelings

He is centre of gravity in our lives, we see our childhood in him
He is our heart beats and purpose of our lives. I see vision of God in him

He is darling of his parents and reasons for our smiles
We wait for his arrival from school daily, his arrival vibrates

What to say of his innocence, way of talking to us and care for us
Though he is just 6yrs but my best friend, he loves his Nany and Mama

Our prayers to God may he become a responsible human being
And be source of joy to his parents and all his loved ones. AMEEN

By Mamutty chola

How Long This Shadow Of Gloom

There are some whose lives remain under gloom for ever
Left alone, neither any loved ones to care for nor friends

Whom he trusted as his destiny turned out be his nemesis
All ditched him in his hours of crisis like floating clouds

Stress is so acute; he wonders why not to disappear into oblivion
To escape from the hell, it has been since ages with no rays of hope

He had sown saplings of roses; to spread happiness in his life
Alas! except one sapling rest turned out to be cactus in his life

He has lost the will and desire to go on living in the hell
Still for the sake of loved ones, he lives on with tsunami within

His life is like a lost traveler in the vast desert all alone
He has since reconciled with his loneliness as his destiny

For the loved ones he sacrificed everything, now they are his biggest tormentors
His mistakes of the moment committed in emotion resulted in never ending misery.
Had never visualized such would be the penance for his folly in life

Have a message for all; never make promises or take decision
When either you are very happy or very sad in life else will live to regret rest of your life

Remember people come to our life either as blessing or as curse Loved ones being part of us, **we have to accept them as** our destiny!!!

By Mamutty chola

BLESSED ARE THOSE IN LOVE

Years have gone by, I couldn't forget
Those tears filled eyes of my love
For no reason I am feeling sad today
Only hope she is fine with her loved ones

If you want to understand then listen
God neither resides in Ayudhya nor in Kaaba
God is one whichever name you call him
He is omnipresent and within you and me
Soul's presence within us is proof of God

The day your memories come to dominate
your dreams, take it from me it is sign of
your giving up life. Be on guard

If you speak truth each and every time
You are not required to remember any thing

Do you know to sink, you need life? for that
Reason only dead bodies float on water

Listen to me, never worry, worry is like a
debt, which you do not owe to any body

It is always a pleasure to lose if the winner
happens to be your loved ones

It is you and you only my love, you
Understood me and gave me the
feelings of being loved for my sake

Nothing will change even if I am gone,
many came before me and disappeared
into oblivion but show goes on; it is life.

By Mamutty chola

I LOVE NATURE AND LIFE

I love life but I hate narrow-mindedness
I hate discrimination, and intolerance

But
I love nature and its splendid wonders
The morning cool breeze, carefree birds flying in the sky
The flow of majestic rivers, the miles of miles spread green fields
The mighty sea waves giving message of life to humanity

The glorious high ice covered mountains kissing the sky
The heavenly caravans of floating clouds in the sky
The mysterious wonder called solar systems
The enchanting moon, glaxy of stars and planets

The all-powerful sun and its benevolent gift of light to humanity
The beauty and magical impact of Moonlight during full moon
I love, adore and communicate with galaxy of stars
I Love thorns for its concerns for flowers in the gardens

I love speed, enjoy careless floating charms and beauties of life
I admire the mutual devotion of the butterfly and candles
I love the blooming beauty and fading youth amidst us
I feel the joy of meeting, the also mourn demise of loved ones

The union and separation of lovers in youth fantasy
The lifelong promise of togetherness and breaks up
The tension of hate and joy of love
The events of new birth and death of the old

The 24 by 7 struggles for existence and regrets of missed opportunities
The pang of destruction and joy of construction
The ruins of war and celebration of victory
I am crazy of nature's bounty and rejoice it

I believe life is action and inaction is death
To live to make the world realize value of our lives
To live life as an example of live and let live
To make my present proud of my past deeds

To work always on the strengths of others
I am aware that time is the great game changer
Time is everything, power, wealth and our existence
Time is free gift to humanity to avail of and excel in life.

By Mamutty chola

LOVING MEMORIES

He still waits for his lost love despite
Ages gone by like fleeting seasons

He still cherishes a found hope
Deep down in his valley of heart

He still remembers her as ever before
In his hours of loneliness when all alone

It has been ages, destiny took her away
Despite lapse of time, she lives within him

Their souls still meet unrestricted
Like all rivers merge into seas

Their souls still enjoy the sea shore
Where they spent time together

The waves still remember them
Keep asking him where is his love

That tree which would give shelter
Still waits for them in silence

Their souls fly high together
Be with lovely clouds and rain

Magic Of Love Is Infinite

One day after long long gap came
Her letter but was blank with drops of tears

The message of her silent love for him
Like other true love, they were not destined

He knows his love is ageless will remain
Young and youthful as fresh like Olive tree.

By Mamutty chola

I Love   Sea Waves

Since my childhood I have had great fascination for sea waves
Each time sea waves come and go back with determination to return

This struggle of waves have been going on since time immemorial
Waves had never got tired nor will ever get tired of till eternity

Waves have been and will be great source of inspiration for humanity
In their struggle for existence, survival and conquering new frontiers.

Being an islander, Andamans, in my fight from obscurity to corporate world
Sea waves were one of the major inspirations for me to tide over the hurdles in life.

In their struggles to cross over the shore they lose their patience and turn into tsunami
Which brings about destruction and misery to people; message is patience too has limit

Unfortunates are the sea waves, their failures give inspiration to the people who have lost hope in live but if waves succeed, that is the end of their existence.what an irony success invites end to their existence.

It is indeed beyond human intelligence to fathom nature's mystery
We men have not been gifted with that faculty of mind to discover nature's mystery.

By Mamutty chola

WINE AND MAN

Man's relation with wine is as old as human civilization
Has been a great company in solitude, distress and stress

For nothing; wine has been blamed since ages like candle
Butterfly takes pleasure in consigning itself to candle flames

Still candle is blamed for the death of the butterfly
If one gets drawn oneself in wine to escape from life's reality

How can one blame wine for one's misery in life?
Despite all religions prohibit drinking as unethical

Still we find wine occupying prime place in our celebrations
If one takes wine as enjoyment, it is soul lifting feelings

One good quality of wine which is admirable is that
Whosoever gets drunk, shall always speak the truth!!

One will never get answer to one's problems
If one gets drunk just to forget one's worry

All will be in vain, in self-control lies the solution
Excess of everything is bad whether love or hate

Only fool blames wine for his misery and helplessness
Remember always neither wine nor barman is to be blamed

If one wishes to enjoy wine, soar high in imagination
Always treat wine as your beloved, you will see its charisma

It is fact of life for all time to come till eternity
Wine shall remain part of our lives till eternity.

By Mamutty chola

Souls Separated

Beyond good and bad far away behind the horizon
I shall wait for you today, tomorrow and forever; my love

Eager to know the song, joy, bliss and beauty of the soul
Watch the morning dew, breeze, crystal streams and floating clouds

Meeting of long separated souls in the valley of love
Their silence speaks, they do not; lost in each other's

Those take love as fun and games, ignorant of true love
Real love is rooted in souls; a reflection of divine bliss
Lovers surrender; ever ready to sacrifice for each other
Even if destiny separates them, they remain in each other

Saga of true love lives on being immortal even after death
Soul being immortal love is ever green and beyond age and time

True love is above all prejudices, customs and religious bigotry
Sad to see lovers are separated; bigots are raising holy war against love

People in love respect love regardless of age; must oppose bigots of
Hate and destroy their regressive values being product of wrong heritage

Books are not mere books they are mirrors of human souls
Depicting saga of love down the ages; love unites and hate divides!!

By Mamutty chola

Soul Is Supreme

Human soul loves nature's creation
Soul by nature and instinct is romantic

That is the reasons we are in love with nature's creations
Be it enchanting scenery, soul soothing music or Sight of rising sun

Be it immortal painting, sculptures, smiles of beloved
Be it majestic flow of crystal streams, ice covered mountains,

Be it lush green forest, scenic wonder of sea waves and beaches,
Be it birds in the sky, kissing the clouds, morning dew and breeze

Be it miles and miles spread rice and paddy fields, roaming animals
Be it dancing peacock, jumping deer's, emperor like lion with families,

Be it shining full moon, galaxy of stars 'the wonders of solar systems
Be it temple and church's bells, or calling of faithful from mosque

Be it young girls on the swings, boys swimming in the rivers in the country side
Be it young lovers hand in hand walking under the tree and meadows and on beaches

Be it spring, Autumn, winter, summer and never ending rains
Be it children dancing in rains, old couples enjoying rains sitting on verandas.

Be it happiness, sorrow, death birth, failure and success despite these, lives flow is on. Soul does not believe in surrender.
But for soul this world have been a desert bereft of beauty and love.

By Mamutty chola

EYES NEVER TELL LIE

If you wish to feel the feelings of your beloved's soul
Look deep into the eyes of your love, which always speak

When she is speaking to you, look into
Her eyes to feel her **feelings; eyes speak her feelings**

Those who forget their love for the beloved
Such love is transient not rooted in soul

Love rooted in soul even after they are parted by destiny
They remain in each other till eternity since soul is immortal

Words are not mere words for those in love
Words unite the two unknown souls in one

Far away beyond the horizon, we shall meet
Alone away from the evil eyes of the world. Shall wait

Oh my love, when I said my life is everything for me in the world
You suddenly became agry; how innocent you are, it is you who is my life!!

By Mamutty chola

LOVE IS CARE

Secret of successful marriage lies
In giving unconditional love to your partner

When you care for others happiness
That is positive sign you do care for others

Objectives of life should be to love all
But trust few and never harm others

A heart which is empty of love for others
Is like a garden never experiences spring

A love bereft of forgiveness is not a love
A forgiveness devoid of love is no forgiveness

A caring life always filled with love for the others
Share happiness with all besides your loved ones

A real and trusted friend is one who is
Available in your hours of need more

A real friend is not one who comes on your death
A real friend is one who does not allow you to die

People in love can see what
Others cannot see or feel in life

When you meet people meet them with smiles
Smile is sign of love emanating from your soul

In life, if you are in love that is the biggest bliss
And being loved and live for your loved one's happiness.

By Mamutty chola

Where Are You My Love?

Since destiny separated us years ago
I have been searching for my love

My eyes have been looking for her
Everywhere, hoping to find my lost love

Been asking the morning breeze
The birds flying high in the sky

Asking the flowers in the garden
Asking the trees and its dancing leaves

Asking the dancing deer and peacocks
Serene river and its singing boatman

Also majestic floating clouds in the sky
Musical rains and its enchanting beauty

Full moon and its romantic charm
Burning candle and dancing butterfly

All said no, not seen anywhere my love
Lost all hopes, came and sat on the sea shore

Sea waves were touching my feet
And telling yes they would often see her

She would come often and sit for hours
Waves were once our confidant

Will wait for my love till eternity
Though separated still she is within me.

By Mamutty chola

NEVER BREAK THE TRUST

All small things get merged into big things
The way all rivers get merged into ocean

Show affection and love to dear ones while alive
On death even adversaries express condolences

What to talk of the depth of love of my beloved
While separating she took away my smile along

When bad time comes it is experienced
Those whom you considered yours, leave you alone

Patience is a warrior, can defeat all adversaries
So never give in, tough time never lasts

My love, I never doubted your love for me
Now be loyal to him, he is your destiny

Knowing your past he has accepted you
Never break the trust, once broken, never be repaired.

By Mamutty chola

BE FAITHFUL TO YOUR PARTNER IN LIFE

Often I wonder over the mystery of our heart
It gives love and hatred being a single heart

Life is a sojourn , meet with smile whomever you meet
No one knows on which turn life's journey will come to an end

For nothing death is ill-known despite her certainty
Unlike love, death has never failed in her appointment

Memories never die nor fade away with time
Always remain with us till our last day on earth

Life has taught me unforgettable lessons
World is selfish and its focus is on self interest

If you live your life in memories of your lost love all along
You will become a prisoner of your memories; for nothing

All these promises of undying love, and loyalty are nothing
But fleeting clouds in the sky; be faithful to your partner in life.

By Mamutty chola

MOTHER EARTH'S CRY

I love not only human beings
I love nature in totality

Be it dancing leaves on trees
Be it paddy fields spread over

Be it morning breeze and its coolness
Be it mighty dancing waves in the sea

Be it dancing peacock and deer
Be it majestic lion and their herds

Be it birds flying above in the sky
Be it caravans of clouds kissing the icy mountains

Be it crystal streams and waterfalls in the country side
Be it vast rivers submerging into the oceans

Be it sights of morning and evening sun rise and sun set
Be it flowers in the gardens and butterflies dancing

Be it first rain with musical sound all around
Be it the sight of moonlight in the full Moon

Be it magnificent sight of the solar systems in the night
Be it vast deserts and its ever changing dunes and features

I can sense and feel the silent cry of nature's creations
We ,in our greed for development, are on the path of self-destruction

If not checked our mother earth will turn into an inferno
Then we will realise, we cannot eat money.

By Mamutty chola

What Is The Reality Of Soul?

People come and go, we
Do not know where they go

This journey of coming and going
Is on since birth of Adam and Eve

Like time, one who departs never comes back
All religion say the soul is immortal

Some talk of day of judgement some immortality
Death ushers in end of one's life on this earth

Like sun sets but rises again each morning
We human have been in search since ages

To know the secret of life and death since
Dawn of human civilization and still on

But nature has not gifted humans
the faculty of mind to discover and understand
the mystery of nature's power

Ho man! how ignorant you are in your
Short sojourn on earth wasting your life

To unravel nature's power; rest assured,
you would fail says the saga human
struggles down the ages.

By Mamutty chola

LONELINESS VS SOLITUDE

WE ENJOY NATURE'S BEAUTY IN SOLITUDE
BE IT MOON AND STAR, FLOATING CLOUDS

LONELINESS IS ALWAYS WITH YOU
WHEN YOU ARE WITHOUT A COMPANION

WHEN THE WHOLE WORLD IS VICTIM OF LONELINESS
HOW CAN ANY ONE ESCAPE FROM THE CURSE OF LONELINESS

THERE IS DIFFERENCE BETWEEN LONELINESS AND SOLITUDE
LONLINESS IS A CURSE WHEREAS SOLITUDE A BLESSING

SOLITUDE WHEN YOU ARE BUSY IN CREATIVE JOBS;
WRITING POETRY, OR LOST IN SOLVING HEALTH ISSUES

ONE CAN BE LONELY ANY WHERE IN DAILY LIFE
BE IT AT HOME, OFFICE, WHILE TRAVELLING IN TRAIN

ONLY THOSE WHO COULD FACE LONELINESS
CAN ONLY OVERCOME LONELINESS IN LIFE

EVERY ONE IS A VICTIM OF LONELINESS
SINCE BIRTH TO DEATH WITHOUT EXCEPTION

ALOOFNESS UNDER THE SOLITUDE IS SOUGHT BY THE PERSON
WHEREAS IN LONELINESS IT IS CURSE IF NOT HANDLED; CAN BE FATAL

THE SOLITUDE IS A PREREQUISITE FOR ANY INVENTION, CREATIVITY
HUMAN CIVILIZATION IS INDEBTED TO SOLITUDES FOR ITS BLESSING.

BY MAMUTTY CHOLA

DREAMS REALIZATION

Life is not in search of self: self-awareness
Life is an ongoing invention of self-realization

Never view life from other's perspectives
View your life's dreams in your mind screen

Life is nothing but your experience
I consider wisdom sum total of experience

All have to die it is our destiny
But few; lucky to lead happy life

Never live a life of others
Neither compel others to live your life

Always remember, no substitute for character
Fame, is transient always like season

Never search for love; instead
Remove all the barriers within you

Let your internal beauty glow and shine
Must for you to share beauty in others

Those who are guilty of injustice.
Never expect justice from them!!

Do and die is a slogan of by gone era
Do and share joy is the mandate of new era

It is not important where you are in life today
What is important; are you on the right path?

Never rest on your past laurels, change being permanent, success is a journey not a destination.

By Mamutty chola

HOPE CREATES FUTURE

Life is not indebted to you
You first deserve then desire

If you aspire to fly beyond the horizon
Develop the capability like that of falcon

Hope is that bird which takes you to the land of bliss
Away from misery, suffering and deprivation

Despite endless challenges and wickedness
This world of our is worth living, if you are honest

In the womb of imagination and dreams live
Hidden in the caravans of happiness; find it

Never give up hopes; setbacks are passing phase
Without hope you are like bird without wings

Believe me, I love darkness for its hidden beauty
But for darkness, how could I enjoy eternal beauty

The galaxy; the abode of Moon, stars and planets
Fleeting dark clouds in full Moon with its charms

The day gone is past, day to come is a mystery
Today is reality, your hope is buried in today

Time gone never comes back unlike season
Time whether good or bad it never lasts

Hope is a waking dream in reality
Let your dream be your focus and destination

Lucky are those who do not aspire in vain
They believe and have faith in their actions

While alive, whatever you do for self will go with you
Whatever you do for humanity, will live long after you are gone.

By Mamutty chola

MAGIC OF POSITIVE THOUGHT

What are you, you are nothing
But your thought and action

Every day can be good or bad
All depend on your thought and action

Every day can be better and the best
Your focused action can make the day better and best

All great inventions are results of
Positive thoughts and actions

Any person can change his future
If thoughts and attitudes are positive

Positive thought can illuminate heart and mind
Which will transform person into enlightened soul

Become an example for the world and not lesson
Be a source of inspiration for the aspiring.

By Mamutty chola

THAT STANGER

I often would see a stranger daily on my evening walk
Sitting on the bank of the river all alone gazing at river's flow

It seems he had been through many ups and downs in life
His face was the index of his sufferings; under gone

He would keep watching the flow of the rivers in solitude
He would keep indulge in soliloquy looking at river's flow

Thought of talking to him and find out his reason for aloofness
Seeing me looking at him, he asked why I was so keen in him

He said his life had been saga of tragedy, misfortune and loneliness
He said life was like river's flow, never stopped like time

Change was only permanent rest all transient
What he said was a reality like sunlight

I came thinking those who fail to keep pace in life
Would find themselves thrown into oblivion

Come what may never lose hope and never give up
You are not defeated till you quit.
All difficult times are passing phase like river's flow

Neither time nor adversities are permanent
We all have to be positive in life and have trust in self.

Life's principles are different, it tests you first and give lesson later
So invents capabilities like water not that of stones.

By Mamutty chola

Our Musical Earth

This earth of ours is musical orchestra
Did you ever realise or feel the feelings

This moon and its enchanting moonlight
These shining stars with its magical spell in sky

The grandeur of Sun rise and sun set
The majestic dancing waves in the ocean

The romantic morning breeze in spring
The dancing leaves of the giant trees

The carefree birds flying amidst fleeting clouds
The miles and miles stretched greenery all around

The dancing peacock and deer in the forests
The musical rains and its drops falling on trees and roof tops

The enchanting melodious song of boatman in river
The sound of drums and melodies of village girls

The sweet sound of Aazaan from the Mosque
The musical sound of bells from temple and church

The soul enriching guruwani from ghurduwara
The recital of devotional songs by Sufi saints from Darga.

My prayers to all do not destroy our earth for greed
This earth of ours is the gift of nature to humanity.

Protect it, nourish it, let it bloom like spring bloom
So that we can hand over a better earth to next generation.

By Mamutty chola

LONELINESS OF MY HEART

Seen in garden flowers and thorns
Live in harmony unlike we human beings

Being human, we live like adversaries and enemies
There always exists trust deficit like two banks of a river

Had a chance to look into mirror after a long gap
Face to face in front of mirror, saw a known stranger

Saw far off hutment set on flame
Asked self why again this destruction

Came message few more hutment set on fire
By forces of darkness, ignorant, intolerant and hatred

What an irony whom I would consider others
Saved my life from communal frenzy and madness

After along gap, I saw the intolerant in the temple
What made him to think of God for atonement

There was light all around except in my house
Thought of giving shelter to darkness for a night!!

The one who was once very close to my heart
When met by chance behaved like a stranger

Where these talks of we vs they would take us
Need to ponder ask self, who are responsible?

People often talk of solitude of vast desert
No one cares to know the loneliness of neglected millions!

By Mamutty chola

BONDAGE OF PAIN

The relief and solace I received at Bar
Never received either in Mosque, temple or church

The bonding and empathy for each other's in Bar indeed
Was missing in mosque, temple and church; say the distressed

For that reason, only you would find all rejected souls in bar
For they receive love, care and peace in each other's company

What a pass we come to, agnostics question existence of God in statues
some misguided say which ever statue they pray to; would turn into God.

By Mamutty chola

INFINITE WAIT

Despite ages, she still lives within me
Like an angel guiding me all the time

She would come like fairy in spring bloom
When she would speak, was like , music all around

When her beautiful hair would fly with breeze,
There would be echo of joys all around

Her beauty was no less than of fairy from heaven
Her love for me was deeper than ocean and higher than sky

She would wait for me daily every evening on the sea shore
Those days; spent together were like bliss in heaven

Destiny willed it otherwise and got separated years ago
I still remember our last meeting with her tear filled eyes

Those beautiful memories I have preserved deep down
In the valley of my heart well protected from the evil world.

By Mamutty chola

POSITIVE THINKERS ARE VICTORS

*S*easons do come back
Sun and moon do rise
Solar systems radiate sky
Morning cool breeze brings bliss along
Springs and rains rejuvenate meadows
Birds of various types dominate the sky
Majestic march of caravan of clouds
Are delights to watch at dawn or sunset
Buds blossom into flowers in the gardens
But there are some unfortunate souls
Despite amidst crowds remain lonely
They wander aimlessly all alone in vast desert
Like dust always remain at the mercy of the wind
Their lives are like stormy waves in the sea
They are like boats caught up in whirlpool of tsunami
Despite residing by river side remain thirsty all life
They forget happiness and sorrow are inseparable
Oh man nature's justice is unfathomable for all creatures
Do you know why some flourish and many whither away
Everything rests on your thought; thinking is real arbiter of life
So we say thinking makes all difference; some become Hitler and Gandhi!!

By Mamutty chola

YEARS AGO

My love, It has been years ago destiny separated us
I still feel your absence despite years since lapsed
My love, it is impossible to forget you despite lapse of years
Like a olive tree, your memory **has been ever green in my mind**

There is no denial none like you were for me in this world
My love, you and you only are in my heart beats

How can I forget those beautiful time spent together
When I sit and reflect, I feel it has been only like yesterday

Your love and commitment had been unmatched for me
Till the last day of our togetherness, we were like one soul in two bodies

Very thought of you brings back those unforgettable days
You never ever got angry despite my mistakes once in a while

Separation by cruel acts of destiny were not less than a death
But your loving memory and last promise to keep smiling

Made me face the dark moments of never ending loneliness
With fortitude. You are and shall ever remain an inspiration

You, my love is always in my prayers and shall remain so
May God keep you always smiling as you took away my smile as token of our love!!

By Mamutty chola

Why Soul Is Sad Today

I very often go and would sit on the sea shore
Often indulge in soliloquy with waves dashing at my feet

Many a time while lost in thought, I would slip over stones on the path.
There a comes voice, ho man! Be attentive while walking

What a wonder, even the stones lying on the path are concerned
Whereas we men have least concerned for fellow human beings

Many a times I have experienced hopes turning into frustrations
Watched with helplessness, patience and silence as bystander

At times lost in past memories while alone
Find her reflection wherever I look when alone

This unspeakable sadness and melancholy not without reasons
Reasons not known to self, still soul has a feeling of gloom

What to talk of my sense of ecstasy and absent mindedness
When I look into mirror, I find reflection of my love!

By Mamutty chola

APPEARANCES ARE ALWAYS DICEPTIVES, MIND YOU

Never form opinion based on first impression
Each person carries a tsunami within him known to
Self but unknown to others!
Here I wish to narrate an incident experienced by me
Way back in 1988 when I was in Oxford UK
One of the weekends I was waiting for train at Metro station.
There was a man with his little son sitting next to me on the bench.
The little guy was constantly showing tantrums and creating
Nuisance for others. The father was lost in his thought unmindful of
His son's nuisance. There was another man who was unable to withstand The child's tantrums and told the father in rude tone can't you discipline your son? Don't you see your son has become a nuisance for others?
The father gave him a hard look and said sorry for being disturbed by my son
Do you know something said the father, the child has lost his mother yesterday for cancer.
Suddenly the atmosphere of hostility, and apathy towards the father turned into Empathy. The man became apologetic for his rude behaviours.
The moral of the story; never jump to the conclusion otherwise the conclusions would jump on you.!!

By Mamutty chola

Oh My Love

Ho my love forgets, we ever met
Better to forget each other ever met

Henceforth; my heart will not beat for you
What should I say to you my love?

I set you free from all your promises of
Lifelong company; together till death

My prayers and good wishes
for you shall ever be for you

Will always cherish the days
spent together deep down in my heart

Will never, ever be cause for your embarrassment
As I am fully aware of your circumstances and plight

The barriers between us of customs and religion
Are so high it is impossible for me to challenge

You are like Moon above in the sky; even if
I try to reach like falcon in the sky, I will fail

The destiny has willed it otherwise
We are like two banks of a river; will never meet.

By Mamutty chola

OUR COUNTRY -- INDIA

This country of ours belongs to all Indians
Our country is confluence of composite culture
Of Hindu, Muslims. Christens, Sikhs, Jain and Parsi

India is known for its tolerance and unity in diversity
Many caravans came over the centuries and settled down in India
Even those who came as conquerors adopted this land as their home
And decorated India with magnificent monuments like Taj Mahal
Red ford, Shalimar Park, Jama Masjid, Char Minar, Kutab Minar,
And many more as. expression of their undying love

India is land of Buddha, Kabir, Guru Nanak,Mahaveer,Ameer Khusro
Among the historical figures like Ashoka, Akbar, Mahatma Gandhi
Nehru, Sardar Patel. Indira Gandhi, and Ambedkar the architect
our constitution,

We are proud of our democracy and democratic institutions
and enjoy universal acclamation and the unifying force of
unity in diversity; the very idea of India

India's rivers like Krishna, Godavari, Bharamputra,Ganga jumana.
Sutlej Beas are abode of Indian culture and civilization for thousands
of years.

The majestic Himalayas on the north, Vast desert in the west and
Magnificent Arabian sea in the west, Indian ocean in the south
and Bay of Bengal in the east are gift of nature to India.
All round greenery spread miles and miles with enchanting meadows

And ice covered mountains kissing the sky, a breath taking beauties indeed!!

*Melodious songs in spring from village girls on the swings and boatmen from river are treats to the eyes, early morning call from mosque for the faithful,Guruwani
from guruduwara, enchanting sound of bells from temple and church are reflection of Indian's secular and
tolerant cuture of live and let live .*

*India, has passed through many stages of her history of Oppression, slavery , monarchy , autocracy but has since mastered in the art of democracy as beckon of hope for the oppressed world over.
We as nation have woken up and are on the path of excellemce with determination to conquer new frontiers beyond moon and stars in the heavenly
planets awaiting human arrival.*

By Mamutty chola

MY LOST LOVE

Whenever I am alone there comes rushing old memories
Of my lost love; her very image takes me to valley of bliss

My longing for her is eternal though the destiny parted us apart
My waiting for her is endless that was the promise I had given her

My eyes are always on the lookout for my love wherever I go
Hoping destiny may smile at me once again; but all in vain

My loneliness is sad for me, but memories give company
And often ask me why I am lost always like a traveler in the desert

Both my loneliness and memories reassure me they would never leave me.
They can't see me suffer in solitude all by myself

I consoled my loneliness and memories and said that
I have the company of my love; she comes in my dreams

Her love for me is undying, each time she comes ; says
Never feel I am alone. Take care, our love is immortal

We will meet again on the day judgement
Never to be separated that hope is eternal.

By Mamutty chola

BROKEN DREAMS

Who knows better than me the pains of broken dreams
When dreams for loved ones and self are shattered for reasons of myself folly

Trusted those who were enemies in friend's guise
My folly of trusting them blindly resulted in self destruction

Had never thought even in my worst dreams such day would come with chain of events hidden with misfortunes and never ending problems

As saying goes, if we trust someone and reposed faith
End results; we will either get a good friend or a good lesson

There was a time, happiness and joy were at my command
and I was grateful to God for His benevolence

Lady luck is knocking at my door with her benevolent smile
Soon I will be liberated from the confinement of misfortune

I know my atonement and hard work will not go waste.
Life rewards only deserving and not needy; I am destined for better days again.

All successes are like transient camps because change is only permanent, rest all are like fleeting clouds and running streams

I trust in self and have a focused vision beyond horizon. I believe action is life and inaction is death; it has been the saga of human lives.

By Mamutty chola

PILLOW AS CONFIDANT

Pillow is matchless and unparalleled as confidant
Never betrays the trust reposed in it by confidant

Never find a single example of betrayal by pillow
Of its confidant in human history since dawn

An eternal companion and co-traveler of broken hearts
And a refuge in all, situations for the rejected souls.

Pillow is unknown to betrayal, fraud, and cheating
Its existence is truth, loyalty, reliance and trust.

Pillow empathizes with dejected, uncared for and unfortunate
Souls like refuge, shelter and like caring mother in life.

How I wished, we humans had the sublime qualities of pillow in us
Then our world would have been a cradle of love and peace.

Neither there would have been separation from the loved ones nor
Bitterness in life; if we had learned to lead a life like that of pillow
in life!!!

By Mamutty chola

GIFT OF LOVE

True love refreshes our soul
Give hopes for living

life blossoms with its enchanting beauty
Life finds meaning in its existence when in love

My love, you are centre of my life
You are my first and last love

I am grateful to God for HIS benevolence
All desires fulfilled with your presence in my life

Your beauty is matchless like an angel
Those beautiful eyes of yours remind me

Of serene lake shining in full moon
How I wish I could remain drown in it

Lucky are those who are in love and being loved
Those innocent souls live like single soul in two bodies

I love my life and love the world, share joy
With one and all unmindful of customs and social prejudices

Love unites and hate divides
Love gives life, hate takes away life

True love is God and those innocent souls
United by love find images of God in each other

Ho Love!, my love for you is deeper than the oceans,
Taller than the Himalayas and stronger than the time,

My love is eternal, rooted in soul not in your fleeting charm
I fell headlong in love with you for your character and grace

One message of life I wish to share with all
Whether love or hate both are blind!!!

By Mamutty chola

Grip Of Sadness

Those who love and be loved
Only assert their claim on each other

Our tears are language of our silence
Which express self both in sadness and happiness

Those who kept pace with time
Found happiness as companion

Never narrate your miseries to others
The world praises only rising sun

Who has time to listen to your miseries
When the world itself is in the grip of sadness

Life means fun, celebration and joy
Whoever understood, could enjoy life

I still remember that tree which would give us shelter
I was told time has absorbed the tree in its existence

There lies buried unfilled desires, hopes and aspirations
Of unknown humanity deep down in the volcano of time; gone by

On canvass of time, leave your mark for posterity
If you wish to attain immortality even after you are gone

Joy and sorrow, success and defeat, fame and infamy
All are transient in life like your sojourn on mother earth.

By Mamutty chola

MARCH OF HUMAN CIVILZATION

Whenever the rulers of the day fail
In the their core responsibility towards
Ruled, revolution is the end results;
A complete change in regime.
Whenever revolution failed it ends in
Mutiny like that of our famous munity
Of 1857 against then colonial British empire.
Whenever the rulers treat their authority as
responsibility in such regimes, instead of revolution
evolution reigns supreme. Example of USA, UK, FRANCE and others.
Under evolutionary process; peace, tranquility and
Social equilibrium are guaranteed in the country.
World history is nothing but saga of revolutions
And evolutions since dawn of the human civilization.
The well tested regimes are those which are
Proactive to the aspirations of the ruled; be it
Democracy or communism.
For that very reasons, regimes like dictatorship,
monarchy, Oligarchy and autocracy are dying
Species from the anal of human history.

By Mamutty chola

Those Memorable Days

Oh my love, I still remember our first meeting
I would wait for your arrival at college bus stop
I found in your smile the message of love
You were different from others like a fairy from heaven

Whenever I would be sad you would embrace with love
You were symbol of love, beauty and grace
It has been ages destiny took you away from me
I still live with hope we would meet once again,

You are in my memory and dreams like soul
My prayers are always for you and your well being
After many years I happened to visit our college city
Our loving memories came flashing in mind's screen

My eyes were searching for you everywhere
Went to the restaurant we would meet very often after college
Went to Marina beach where we would meet often in the evening
When looked around lives were same except I missed you

I went and sat on the sea shore gazing at the waves
Waves were touching my feet and telling me
Where you were all these days; have come after years
I felt waves were complaining for delayed arrival

Felt waves were saying she would come very often and
Sit for hours for you and would go back disappointed
My eyes were eagerly looking for that tree which would
Give us shelter from the scorching heat as good friend

It seemed like our love, the tree had become victim of nature fury
Heard from wind time has absorbed the tree in its existence
Everything were looking different with passage of time
Tears welled into my eyes and rolled down on my cheek

Tears are our companion both in sorrow and happiness
The surrounding, greenery, lush green trees all around had withered
Except few things unchanged like flow of time and mighty sea waves
And the works of architects of bygone era on the rocks overlooking sea

Thought I would know her where about
I asked repeatedly the spring breeze
Morning dew, floating clouds in the sky
Flying birds returning in groves to their nests

Blossoming flowers in the garden,
Dancing leaves on the tall trees
Dancing deer and peacock in the forest
And asked Moon on full moon night

Crystal water in the streams and flow of river
Also asked falcon high above in the sky
Asked musical rains, burning candle
Asked the galaxy of stars and setting sun

All said they have not seen my love any where
Totally lost all hopes I came and sat on the sea shore
The waves were our confidants for years
I was totally lost about her where about

I was sad and sorrowful sitting on sea shore
Lost in past beautiful memories like tree shade
Asked waves who were our confidant of years
Return those foot prints of my love they preserve

Magic Of Love Is Infinite

Replied the waves those footprints of your love
Are now part of their existence for years?
Like my memories of my love, the relation
Between memories and love inseparable

Living with eternal hope destiny will unite us
The time spent together will remain alive
Been a source of inspiration for me to live on
She came as angel and taught the meaning of life

Despite difference of religion, we were one
Love is secular. Love unites never divides
The longing for her will remain eternal
Her memory I have preserved deep down in heart

How I wished I could tell what she means to me
And her magic on my life despite being away
When I think of her beautiful eyes like calm lake
Lips like rose petals, hair like dark clouds in the sky

It has been years I am with my loneliness
Despite years gone by, there is no end to my solitude
Years may lapse but my wait is eternal for my lost love
Her very thought inspires me to live; love being rooted in soul

I know she must be thinking of me in her solitude
Else why should I have this undying urge for her
Will ask almighty on the day of judgement why
This to me; I know love demands sacrifice

When it comes to her beauty and grace
Words fail me to describe her angel like grace
Sea waves still miss her and call her
They still remember our undying love for each other

When I look at full moon I would see her reflection
At times I feel she is still part of my existence and
Would come and knock at the door with usual smile
Knowing; she is no longer part of me since years

As long as we were together; life was a dream
Her love, care and concerns for me ; matchless
Those stolen moments spent together on sea shore
Those innocent talks of future life together

Unmindful of cruel destiny waiting for its kill
Our travel together in bus to drop her after college
I still remember the day we took leave after college
Will never ever forget those tears filled eyes of my love

Saying come back she would wait for me
But destiny willed it otherwise and parted for good
I had promised her I would live with smile
True love never ages or dies being rooted in soul

Flight of my imagination takes me to known places
Hoping I would meet her at the turn of road
My disappointed hope is still hopeful of
I often find self-lost in her memories when alone

At times I feel my memories are dominant over my dreams
I live rest of my life alone but memory of love is there always
Life would have been a dream sequence if she were with me
She still comes in my dreams and tells me take care she is exceptional

I know for certain, I have to complete the sojourn alone on this earth
She is helpless and I powerless to face the barriers of prejudices
The time spent together now seems like dreams of by gone era
Cruel hands of destiny parted us apart, still we live in each other

When comes to think of true love, true love is eternal
Beyond time and space; only separated love become immortal
Be it Romeo Juliet.,Hira Range, Laila Majnu,Shiri Farhad and
King Edward of UK who renounced his throne for his love- a commoner

My life often asks me why this misfortune with me since long
I console my life it has been the fate of ill-fated **lovers; separation**
Is inevitable for love to become immortal, so why to mourn
My love being immortal, it has been source of inspiration

It has been ages since I had smiled last
Hoping lost love would knock at my door
True love turns man into angel being pure
Lover sees image of God in his beloved

She came as breeze ; took away my smile as token of love
I have become prisoner of loneliness though memory is there
How I spent my loneliness no one is there to ask me how I am
I have been in the midst of despair and darkness since long

There was a time thing was cheerful and pleasant
Happiness, success and love were my companions
If your memories are inspirational, life's journey will be pleasant
Helps people to fight their ways up in life

How can I forget my chance meeting with my love at the airport?
After ages; at first look I could not recognise her
It seemed she had been through bad time since we parted
Neither the charm, nor look, nor that smile or grace on her face

I felt as if she had left behind her beauty in the past
For her also it was surprise to see and meet me after ages
I had never thought we would meet again in life but destiny is destiny
I was searching my lost love in a stranger, when asked how was she

She said life had been in despair and compromises all through
It had been like a prisoner of loneliness in the custody of memory
When she asked me how had been my life since parted
In reply came flood of emotion bursting into uncontrolled tears

Given our family commitments it was next to impossible for us
To start life afresh. I told her people come to our lives
Some as blessing and some as curse both are our destiny
As she was to catch the flight I said goodbye for the last time

I was indeed happy I saw her and her love for me in those sad eyes.

(This is a poem based on my imagination and observation as poet but must be true for millions of souls on mother earth, Happy reading)

By Mamutty chola

ME AND SEA WAVES

When alone I often think of my days spent with sea waves
Our relations have been very close since boy hood

I derive immense peace of mind in solitude on sea shore
I would go to sea for swimming while in school with friends during summer holidays

Today when I was sad and stressed I went to sea shore
They keep inspiring me not to lose hopes giving their own examples

I would succeed if I keep my struggle on like them since ages said waves
Learned from their lives; nothing ventures nothing gains, keep struggles on

Despite years of struggles they have not given up, life is action say waves
I said their advice well taken but I told waves better remain in sea for own safety

Do not all you know they moment you cross sea and land on shore you will die?
I explained to them law of nature , in their success is hidden their death

Waves exist for others and to give inspiration to others for struggle
Waves laughed at my ignorance, ho man, we never die, after crossing the shore

We get absorbed and come back to sea to keep our movement on
This sequence will keep on till eternity as ordained by nature;
waves are immortal!!!

Like sun, moon, stars, planets and wind, till eternity
Revelation by sea waves was indeed a pleasant surprise for me.
By Mamutty chola

MEMORY AND LONELINESS-RELATION

Memory and loneliness are inseparable
They are lifelong companion of each other

Bitter memory is source of unbearable agony
Happy memories are blessing in loneliness

Life is confluence of memory and loneliness
None is exempt from the cycle of loneliness and memory

If the memories are pleasant and inspirational
It provides strengths to fight on in life

Memory can be both pleasant or unpleasant
Success and failures have direct relation to once's action

Taj mahal is symbol of love for humanity
Though built by Shah jahan in memory of his wife

If you have a pleasant memory to rely on
Then even acute loneliness will pass on like time

Soul and body despite being inseparable
While alive, never meet during the life time

Unlike soul and body things are different for
Loneliness and memory, stay together in their silo till death.

By Mamutty chola

LOVE IS BLISS

Despite passage of time, I still miss my love
Many seasons came and went but she never

Morning breeze brings her memory afresh
With her beautiful smile and grace

Morning dew with its melancholy
Reminds me of her tears filled eyes

The dark clouds filled sky remind me
Of her beautiful dark hair dancing with the wind

Her intoxicating eyes remind me of calm lake
Her smiles remind me of blossoming flowers

Her flying scarf brings along
Music all around in the air

When she speaks, life vibrates in ecstasy
Her majestic walk reminds me of deer in the forest

Her beauty and grace remind me of fairy from heaven
She was different from others but symbol of love

She resides deep down in the valley of my heart
Like a beckon of hope and angel of guidance

Separate we did years ago but
Still she is part of my life always.
By Mamutty chola

LOVE AND HATE

If your actions are governed by the code of ethical **and moral**
You can rest assured, happiness and prosperity be at your command

Build your home as abode of peace and love
Like birds who make nests on green and flourishing trees

Our heart is like temple or mosque
Conscience is like chamber of justice

Life is like river on flow; non stop
Like love which is immortal and infinite

The difference between flower fragrance and human goodness
The flower fragrance spreads with wind but human goodness is omnipresent

For success in life qualities required are, attitude, imagination,
Self-confidence, integrity, perseverance and character
Of all; attitude and self-confidence is decisive and final

Unless you have fire in your belly to excel
Attainment of goal will elude you ever and ever

Have you ever thought of difference between love and hate?
Love always gives life and hate always takes life.
By Mamutty chola

Tender Heart

Tried many a times to build my own dream home,
Ill –luck would have it, each time I failed

The adversarial world has made me stone hearted
Any amount of offence does not affect me despite severity of the attack

, Have been unlucky, failed to meet lost love despite long wait
I would wait for her till eternity like mighty sea waves

Love does happen one cannot choose to fall in love
Love is that flame its spark once lighted, never ceases to burn

Deep down in my heart, longing does exist for my love
Her memories keep flashing in my mind's screen when I am alone

As token of love while departing she took my smiles along
It is ages since I have smiled last, I have to live as promised to her

we, human being are bundle of desired and unfulfilled dreams
Whether we live in palace or huts desires are unlimited

This is a part of luggage we carry from womb to tomb
For that reasons there are endless struggles since birth to death

What a hypocrisy being stone hearted person talk of charity
And compassion sound hallows to the core; Ho man be rational.
By Mamutty chola

I Love Life

My sad poetry is reflection of reality
I being part of society, how can I detach myself from reality
Disappointments have been my co-traveler since long
I hate intolerance, narrow mindedness and
Discrimination because I am madly in love with my life

I am crazy about nature bounty, be it morning breeze
Birds flying high in the sky, majestic flow of river,
Dancing crops on lush green field spread over miles and miles
Mighty sea waves inspiring us for struggle
Because I am madly in love with my life

I love and adore the undefeatable falcon flying high in the sky
I love enchanting moonlight during **the full Moon**
I indulge in soliloquy with stars and moon in the sky
I am in love with mysteries of solar systems
Because I am madly in love with my life

I love flowers in the gardens spreading fragrance all around
I am in love with my love's beauty, youth and her magical hair
I love speed in life with its vibrancy and actions
I love and admire sacrifice of the candle and madness of butterfly
Because I am madly in love with my life

I observe fading beauty and irreversible aging of youth
Also celebration of victory and mourning of defeat
Learn lesson from blossoming and withering of relations
I see promise of lifelong company and betrayals
Because I am madly in love with my life

I observe the misery of poverty and pinnacle of progress
Destruction of war and cry for peace all around
I am in love with all creations of nature
I believe life must be lived with joy and fun
Because I am madly in love with my life

Aim of my life is to make other realise
Life is not search of self but inventing of self
Leave a mark on time canvass for posterity
And be a role model for others in life
Because I am madly in love with my life

Treat time as wealth and power
No one can store time for posterity
Time and youth once gone never come back
Keep pace with time change being permanent
Because I am madly in love with my life

Never wait for better tomorrow
Every time is right time for good work
Today is reality. live well today for better tomorrow
Tomorrow never comes says Bible
Because I am madly in love with my life.
By Mamutty chola

LIVE LIFE LIKE SEASONS

Your tears filled eyes speak of
The painful sleepless lonely night of yours

I often wonder, why people betray each other in love
The trust reposed once broken, remains broken till death

Relation in life is built on trust and faith in each other
Any relation without trust and faith is like a castle on sand

The spell of loneliness and sadness when become too long
What hope, what patience what silence all are under gloom

Realization since dawned, all are concerned about self only
One who would say, cannot live without me had gone like floating clouds

Life taught me live life like seasons, change is reality
Never wait for one who left like time gone
Else you would be left all alone in the journey of life
While your sojourn on earth.
By Mmautty chola

Feelings And Emotions

Years ago I had written a letter but could not post
Today when opened after years, found writings still wet!!

After destiny parted us, I realised
How different you were from others

You would be disappointed , if you keep
Relations with weak persons in life

I meet with smile whomsoever I meet
Why to talk of autumn when you are in spring

That dreams of togetherness with love, remained a dream
Now I live in today which is a reality, gone time never comes back

I trust the language of eyes, though silent
Facial expression could be fake and acted!

The world laughs at those who fall, that is the way
Why should anyone save you, you are not a kid!!

The caravan of time never waits for any one
Whether be a king or a pauper, however powerful or weak

I have suffered so much trusting all in vain
My feelings have turned into stone, nothing affects me now.
By Mamutty chola

HAPPINESS IS HIDDEN IN YOUR THOUGHTS

If your thinking process is do and enjoy
Instead of do and die, your attitude
Towards life will be positive
Your thought process will be like
Got trust instead of betrayal in life
Got love instead of hatred in life
Got smile instead of tears in life
Life means celebration instead of mourning
Got friends instead of enemies in life
Remain always successful instead of defeated in life
Remain in the company of the loved ones
Instead of strangers in life
Speed has been hallmark instead of stagnation in life
Remain amidst spring instead of autumn in life
Enjoyed the songs of life instead of melodies of loneliness
My abode has always been in the garden of love instead of
Traveller in the vast empty desert amidst mirage in life
Reasons, I believe action is life and inaction is death
I believe in living in today; a reality not in future a mirage
My message time and circumstances are harbingers of changes
All successes and failures are transient; keep pace with changes
Only reality; rest all are like floating clouds. Excellence is journey
Not a destination!!
By Mamutty chola

STILL WAIT FOR THY WELFARE

It is a reality we cannot meet even if we wish
It is also a reality our love is immortal

Else the urge to think of you always
Down the years would not have been there

In the years of solitude since we parted
Your thoughts have been my eternal companion

Shall not forget for minute till last day of
My sojourn on the mother earth

I want you to remain happy and smiling
wherever you might be. The time spent,

though very short, in each other company
dreaming of life together Still remain ever green

like an olive tree immune to seasonal effect.
Just wish to know your welfare if read this poem

Our love being rooted in soul resides beyond
horizon in the realm of bliss. I shall await.

By Mamutty chola

Who Has Seen Tomorrow?

Got betrayal instead of loyalty
Got hared instead of love

Got tears instead of smiles
Got disappointment instead of happiness

Got separated instead of union
Got loneliness instead of togetherness

Got setbacks instead of success
Got Autumns instead of springs

Got pains instead of songs of joy
Got emptiness instead of love of loved ones

Despite all these, I have still an urge to live on
Today is reality, who has seen tomorrow?

Life gives equal opportunity to all, if not equality!!!
Be it king, rich, poor or destitute while on sojourn on earth!!

By Mamutty chola

WORLD WITHOUT LOVE IS A TOMB

She came like a morning breeze in my life
Went away like a floating cloud with winds
It has been ages I am in wait. Many seasons came
And went with passing caravan of time

The days spent together will remain ever green
In the deep valley of my heart till eternity.
Very often I would go and sit on sea shore
Where we spent time together dreaming future together

Sea waves were our confidants. When asked to return
The foot prints of my love stored in their hearts
They all replied in unison, that being part of their
Existence, they would not part with. What an unifying

Force love is. Ho! My love when I look at the
full moonlit night in the sky I see your reflection in moon, and stars
Which world can't see except me. No words to express
Pains of separation and loneliness and solitude of years

Being left alone like lost traveller, in a vast desert.
Your memories are always there like an inspiration in my life
Sunsets and sunrises again and moon appears in the sky,
seasons keep changing be it spring, autumn, summer or rain
Nothing interests   me when you are not part of me,
My eyes keep looking for you but you are no where
Do you know that tree we would take shelter in hot summer?
When asked the wind, informed, that tree too has merged with time

I still love life since I have a promise to keep made to you
but I cannot smile, You took away my smile as token of love long ago
While parting for the last time after college. we are now like

Two banks of a river which are never destined to meet
My love for you is eternal but destiny willed otherwise
I will cherish those musical and magical moments of
life spent together as most valued treasure of my life

The journey of my life after we parted been like a journey on fire
The time spent in loneliness are beyond expression for its pain
Your memories captured in my mind's screen will remain fresh
And provide me inspiration to live on to complete my sojourn
on earth.

By Mamutty chola

BONDAGE OF LIFE

Relation between light and darkness
as old as human civilization
Similar to love and hate

Their relations are inter-dependent
If there is no darkness, what use does light have

Nature has created everything in pairs
Like morning and evening

Like tears and smiles
Like happiness and sadness

Like Youth and old age
Like life and death

Like spring and Autumn
Like sky and earth
Like clouds and winds

Like separation and union
Like progress and backwardness

Like heaven and hell
Like rain and sunlight

This is message of God to humanity
There is no such night without a day break

It is true every creature is bound by bondage of love
With one another for that reason all creatures are in pairs.

By Mamutty chola

THE ABYSS IN MY LIFE

You came like spring in my life
Left behind Autumn in my life

The qualities you had,
found in none others

Despite years gone by
you in my mind's screen ever

When alone comes like morning breeze
With joy of music and magical breeze

Lost all hopes of ever meeting you in life
It would be lonely sojourn till my end

I have to live with emptiness and abyss
Your company was journey of bliss

You made me live life with love
The promise given to you be honoured full

My love for you is deeper than ocean
Taller than high above seven skies.

If not this world shall meet in new world
In the meadow of lush green field forever.
Like long separated souls united forever.
By Mamutty chola

Season Comes Back But Not Gone Time

Wish to share words of wisdom
Well-meant critics are really well wishers

Being human it is but natural
To celebrate success with joy

Also necessary to learn from past
Mistakes they are like ladders to success

Never feel sad over past set backs
Sit back and reflect over your happy past

But live in today as if last day
Future is hidden in today's action

Gone time never comes back
But season does come back

Life gives message to all
Life means action, inaction is death

One who would say she was for you
Seen her flying always like floating clouds

Shedding two drops of tears like dew
Her signs of helplessness, being excused

Never to return again
Leaving me in endless wait

This chain of events will go on
Till eternity; uninterrupted while alive

Never become a prisoner of your past
Memory can be companion of loneliness but not of life

Life is not only love for beloved
Live life for loved ones and needy

Live in people's hearts; try once
If you want to be remembered after gone

We all live in our houses being human
Like a sojourn in an inn in life journey.
By Mamutty chola

I LOVE DARKNESS

I love light which provides direction
I love darkness of the night for I can see moon and stars

God's benevolence is unlimited
Every day is good day for good job

Nature's wonder is beyond matchless
From a single seed emerges a big tree

Journey of possible to impossible has been
The reason for all inventions in the world

By walking on meadow gives birth to footpath
Which later transforms into road and highways.
By Mamutty chola

THE LIFE

The loyalty you will always find in broken hearts like treasures in ruins!!
It is not easy to become a good human being because humane quality is very scarce.

Time and circumstance keep changing. Those who fail to keep pace with change are not only reduced to redundancy but irrelevancy in life!! The biggest threats to humanity in the 21st century.

If you wish to earn immortality while alive, try to live in people's hearts
We all live in our homes.

If she had become my partner in life while my sojourn on earth, this life Of mine would have been a dream journey with the company of my love
Alas! destiny willed it otherwise. Now I am like a lonely traveller in vast desert.

Strange are the ways of life, the one who breaks your heart is the one you miss every second of your life .Power of love is invincible
Once in love always in live.

For that reasons separated souls always live in each other even in separation; soul being immortal. For memories are inseparable and remain with us till death.
By Mamutty chola

Song Of Your Memory

This song of your memory brings along
The memorable days spent in each other's arms

How friendly are the caravan of floating clouds?
They come with bliss only, no rain or no storms

Let us live each moment with smiles
There comes day break after each night

The song of memory brings together
Two separated souls after years

Listen to the cry of the oppressed
They want two times meals in life

Never build your dreams home
On the hutment of poor and destitute

Beware of nature fury my friend
Lest you become victim of your wrong doing

The increasing gap between poor and rich is sign of
Impending tsunami lurking from behind the horizon.
By Mamutty chola

Not Destined To Be Mine

Divine rules of creation are so unpredictable
Whom I loved was not destined to be mine

Ho my love! Forget me, don't wait for me
We are like two banks of a river not destined to meet

What an irony men forget God's benevolence
Ho God! I can't forget one whom you created

I am lost in solitude in memory of my love
Neither she came nor I could forget her

There is something very special in my hospitality
Misfortune once comes never leaves me!
I have nothing to give my love except my prayers
May God give all the happiness on earth to you. Ameen.
By Mamutty chola

HEART VS MIND

Oh heart, remain in touch with mind.
Never get inpatient in life.
Being human, one must have desires
But within your limit

Oh heart; do you know realities of life.
Life recognizes deserving ones and not needy.
Deserving gets reward and needy gets charity.

Oh heart; never question existence of God
God is omnipresent, omniscience and omnipotent

Oh heart; you experience, spring, autumn, winter,
rain and summer, happiness, sorrow, and,
Success and failures, There are two sides to everything in life.

Oh heart; never blame your beloved, Love happens
You can't force people to fall in love with you.
Meeting of mind is a pre-requisite.

Oh heart; your biggest problem is that you act first and
Think later unlike mind the very genesis of your problems.

Oh heart; you will always remain in a dilemma. So consult mind
If you wish to be happy in life.

Oh heart; you being abode of love, compassion, pity,
 sacrifice. empathy, sympathy, kindness ,benevolent   and merciful,
you can turn this mother Earth into paradise because love unites.
By Mamutty chola

Pains Of Separtion

Don't be taken in by her innocent look
Ungrateful are always good actors

At each and every turn she meets me
It seems misfortune has developed a liking for me !

There was a time, I had nothing in my life to lose
Since you have come, I am always a sacred of losing you!

People said she was not destined to be mine
Since destiny is God's gift, she is destined to be mine

Destiny does part us as two banks of a river,
But true love lives in each other forever till eternity

Thought of thinking something else today besides you
I am still in dilemma if at all I have to think then what to think

I have serious complaint with my creator as he took you away
Why did't He give me some one like you always caring

Do you know the sign of sad people in life?
Observe closely they smile a lot when with friends!!

By Mamutty chola

Change Or Revenge?

Many tyrants came and disappeared into oblivion
and now resting in their unknown graves since time immemorial
In this mortal world our sojourn on earth is like a transit camp,
Once born death is inevitable.

The recent rise of intolerance and dissent being treated as anti-national are matter of grave concerns. A section of the society is being targeted and told they do not belong to this country. They are different from the majority.

Question is who are they? Are they above constitution?, why are they encouraged to spread hatred in society with immunity and impunity.?
The toxic of hared is poison. Neither the oppressed nor
the oppressors can escape from its fatal consequences.
Any resistance to hate campaign is termed as anti-national!!

How can the oppressed disassociate themselves from their mother land with its? rivers, mountains, the greenery the lush green fields spread miles and miles, the meadows, their birth places the lanes and by lanes, schools, the child hood memories, and friends grown up together?
The morning cool breeze bird flying the sky. It will be like uprooting trees!!
The regime change since last four years and more and their claim of Ache din and inclusive development are nothing bust slogans and frauds

The clamour for change is nothing but revenge of the centuries gone by,!!
Those in power have no sense of history or of true Hinduism. India of today is confluence of diverse culture and civilization. So we say unity in diversity is our strengths. The very idea of India. Those who try to destroy our common heritage TEHZEEB are the real enemies of the country. BEWARE OF THEM.
By Mamutty chola

You Are Always Within Me

There were countless beauties in the world
But you and you only have been my choice

My sad eyes betray my undying love for you
My eyes are my best friend with pains of you

This imprisonment of mine in your love is by choice
Let me remain in prison of your love my love for life

No secret of life can remain hidden till eternity
There is no story which does't have an end in life

Leaving you in my eyes where have you gone my love
Don't you know love does not believe in separation

If you know the art of fathoming tears, my friend
You can read my message of love   in my tears

I am determined to be part of your life journey
Then why this question do I love you, my love

Where you will find a lover like me in the world
Despite being separated for ages, still you live within me.
By Mamutty chola

BEAUTY OF DEATH IS MATCLESS

My heart is feeling lonely for no reason
Hope you are not lonely like me my love

Whether I remain or not, my prayers to God
You remain happy in life wherever you are, my Love

To be with you was my last desire in life, my love
But destiny always did part us apart, my love

You are always in a dilemma to say yes or no to me
When you meet me you always say you are mine

I often try to think something else besides you
But each time I fail to think else once I think of

I had never dreamed of I would be without you ever in life
what a turn of events. Destiny took you away;
left me to suffer alone

World will remain as happy as ever even if we are not there
There will be someone else like us ever to keep the show on

No one can match the matchless beauty of death
When she comes all follow her to the kingdom of unknown.
By Mamutty chola

PANG OF SEPARATION

How can I forget my love
Says inner voice, unless I lose my memory,
 I can't forget my love!!

When you were part of me, time would fly
After separation, time does not move my love

Never raise accusing figure at me my friend
If you have doubt on my commitment, test me

Why should blame you for my pang of separation
It is I who fell in love you are totally innocent

Love all but love her more she
Loves you more than I do

I had heard about a custom but never believed it
After meeting you I realised all are not faithful!!

You never understood nor wanted to understand
I never wanted anything from you but you!

The word we all call life I kept deep down in
My heart since I have named you as my life.
By Mamutty chola

Always Live In Today

Waited in vain for my love.
Alas now left all alone in life
Like lonely traveler in vast desert of life.

Life has since taught me one thing in life
All are concerned only and only in self.

Since her betrayal life was shattered
Like autumn leaves spread and crushed
Under feet by one and all. Still I resolved
To live in the hope of impending spring,

Now when I sit alone and reflect, feel
Guilty for trusting one whom I considered
As my destiny but got betrayal in return.

I have since shut her out of my life;
thoughts, memories and dreams .
I lived a life so far which was impossible to live.

Lesson learned, if you trust someone,
you either get a good friend or a good lesson!!

Live in today. Today is reality. Neither live in
past —a dead yesterday nor in future a fog.
Has anyone seen tomorrow? Give love to
one who deserve your love most. That one is
You my friend. The world exists for you,

You do not exist for the world.
Also remember, no one can force
you to fall in love. Love happens when
meeting of heart and mind happen!
By Mamutty chola

LOVE IS SUPREME

If I were not in love with my love
would have left the pursuit of her
It is not in every body's destiny ,
Love happens, it is a divine gift

My feelings have been in long wait
To feel the feelings of my love
Let me say goodbye to this life
People do remember departed ones

I spent whole life in her memory
Never thought for second for self
What to pen about life; Ho my life
Those who used to be my life
are no longer mine

Life is short, desires unlimited
Acquaintances many, friends limited
Whom to choose as confidant
One who is close but unaware

My love for you is boundless like sky
When asked to mention my last wish it was you
Despite being away, you are within me
How to be with one's love being away,
must learn from you.
By Mamutty chola

Our First Meeting

How can I forget our first meetings years ago?
That first look of her I had been waiting for ages

Came the inner voice she was the one I had been dreaming
I would watch her coming to my college bus stop for catching
Connecting bus daily.

She was very special highly dignified like fairy,
elegant and full of grace.
My life changed since meeting her,
she made me realise what it did mean to be loved

I still remember those beautiful evenings after college on Marina
beach, once in a while long bus trip together to Mahabalipuram

Our short sojourn together is the most memorable days of my life
After college I had to go back to my native place for a short while

Destiny took her away and I lost her for good, But her inspiration
made me struggle in life even for higher studies I went to oxford,
UK.

Her thought has always been with me every second of my life
I did extremely well career wise with her inspiring thought

But there is as abysm and vacuum in my life for ever for her
No one can take her place, it is fact one can't forget ones' first love

Like an engraved gift of rock but for her meeting I wouldn't have succeeded.
I have only one prayer, may God bless her with all the happiness on earth.

By Mamutty chola

LESSONS FROM DEATH

We all curse death.
Is there any who can match
Death in loyalty!!

Death always takes along
Whosoever she meets.

Is there any example in
Human history when
Death has betrayed or
Failed in her commitment ever?

Death is ill known for no reason
For performing her divine duty

Life unlike death gives us
innumerable troubles;
Like hardship, break ups
Hatred, enmity, intolerance
While our sojourn on earth!!!!

Indeed, man is the biggest
hypocrite on earth!
By Mamutty chola

LOVE IS LIFE

In my mind's screen I still see
The tear filled eyes of my love
Though we parted after college for the last time
But she is part of my existence every second

Then why this urge to see her every second
Soul is free from the restriction of our body
Our body is nothing without the company of soul
When I get extremely lonely without her in the night

I try to cover myself with the beautiful thoughts
Of my love to endure endless pang of separation
Whenever she comes in my dreams, always would say, take care
you are not alone, will always be with me in my dreams

I loved her with all the power at my command but
She was not destined to be mine whom to blame for
What a joke destiny has played, she was not to be my destiny
Many many seasons came and went but she never came

I still wait for her how I wished she could come like season once
My soul says my body is a prison, there is no life without soul

My silence and patience are sad for me since ages
They tell better settle down with some one of my liking
Being human it's impossible to live alone, God has made
All creatures in pairs. It is true by living in the
Memory of lost love, I am now left all alone in life!!
By Mamutty Chola

Meadows Of Bliss

One who would recognise me from far off distance
Now pass by as if I am a stranger to her

Since you have decided to say good bye to me
But remember, heart once broken cannot be healed

What is the use in searching for you? you have
since changed, you have not been lost!

Since we have met a new meaning of life
has dawned on me. I now love my life as never before

How can I ever forget you; very thought of you
Takes me too far away land in the meadow of bliss

Oh my love; despite you being away from me
When you think of me then take care of self

Desires, hopes, aspirations and dreams are the
Genesis of human survival on earth; will remain so
till eternity

It has been years' destiny parted us away
she still lives deep down in my heart.
By Mamutty chola

CAN LOVE BE THE CURRENCY OF THE WORLD?

I often dreamed gardens being set on fire in spring
Will any one tell me the meaning of these dreams?

We all accept Ram as our spiritual head of India
Then why this politics in the name of Ram's heritage

Everywhere people are at war on caste or religion
Is this the only way left to survive in the society?

If you can have qualities of falcon within you
You can fly high above the clouds beyond stars

This glittering world have no attraction for me
I am in pursuit of inventing self to know my self

Rule of love can become currency of the world
For it is in the genes of the love to be unbiased and selfless

If the nation is poor and is victim of hunger and poverty
Don't blame the nation, blame the rulers for their greed

Ho fellow countrymen; beware of the lurking danger from
Behind the horizon. Never deviate from the path of tolerance.
By Mamutty chola

NEVER LIVE LIFE WITH EXPECTATION

Oh man, what a pass we have reached you say
whichever statue you worship turns into God!

Oh man, journey of time is on since the creation
of the universe. I too joined the march of infinity
while my sojourn on earth.

Oh my companion, despite living like soul and body
We are still stranger to each other as co-travelers!!
Alas! the one I met and lost like gone time; never to be
my destiny still lives within me.

Oh man,the fame, reputation, status, position and power
Are like rainbow and transient like bubbes in life.
Never forget those misfortunes who look up to you in hopes.
Life means sharing. Never live life with expectation
Remember always givers are the real gainers in life..

By Mamutty chola

BEAUTY OF HUMAN HEART

Heart always acts first think later
Mind always think first, act later

Language of heart is expressed
In feelings, tears and poetry

Heart is so tender like flower
But carries the pains of world within

Mind is available for sale in the market
Heart being invaluable can't be priced

Love in heart being rooted in soul
Is ever green and youthful like olive tree

Heart once broken can't be repaired and healed
Without heart, the beauty of the nature would
Have remained unrecognized and unsung

Heart is repository of love, care, concerned
Sacrifice, has no room for hatred and jealousy

Heart being transparent and open
Can never cheat others unlike mind.

By Mamutty chola

Beauty Of Eyes

A woman's beauty lies in her eyes
Since gateway to her soul is through eyes

To enjoy the beauty of the nature, keep
Your eyes on the Moon, stars and galaxy
And feet on the ground

The beautiful eyes are always on the look out
For love, grace, bliss and togetherness with loved ones

Pure soul filled with love and compassion
Finds expression through beautiful eyes

Our face is an index of mind, eyes through
The language of silence speaks feelings of
Heart and soul

The beautiful eyes of the beloved are like serene lake
Also mirror of her heart and soul

You can close your eyes to reality but not to memories
Which are already saved in your mind's screen till eternity

While talking to any one; be it your loved ones or
professional colleagues, eyes contacts are essential
to feel the feelings.
By Mamutty chola

Bilissful Soul

Soul expresses her presence within us
By our joy, smile, bliss, sadness and melancholy

Our tears are nothing but expression of anguish,
suffering, disappointment, and deprivation of our souls
They are silent cries of our souls

Remember our soul is reflection of us. If you
want your soul to remain in state of bliss
Always thing positive and constructive

Like love, soul loves truth. Our conscience represents soul
For that reason, conscience is called chamber of justice

Real love is rooted in soul, hence immortal
and not in physical beauty which is transient.

If you do rummaging and indulge in inventing self.
Many qualities hitherto hidden in your soul will emerge.

Whether Hollywood or Bollywood actors are paid a fortune
For a kiss and a peanut for soul searching performance!!

By Mamutty chola

Love Is God

The whole world is yours if you are in love and being loved
Those who love themselves can only love the world

If you are heartbeat of your loved ones, it gives you immense
strength being wanted. And if you are in love, it inspires you.

We are born alone, work alone and die alone.
But through your love and friendship you make
It reality that you are not alone when being loved.

Let us always meet others, even if stranger with love and smile
Love can only unite. Love gives life, hate takes life

What loved filled heart can see, one's naked eyes can't see
Like loved filled silence speak, everyone can't hear unless in love

Blessed and lucky are those inspired by love and guided by wisdom
You being the most important person to yourself, love first yourself

Give gift of love to self. Are you aware, how lonely is your loneliness?!
Without love life will be like sunless garden. Love is like sunshine

Rivers merge into ocean, spring season brings bliss
So we say love is truth, love is sharing and love is God.

By Mamutty chola

Tears In Rain

Let me remain where I am
Only ego wants to clamour

Brevity is thy name, ho God,
Your qualities are matchless

How I wished, I had a friend
who could read my tears even in rain

Why people fall in love when
It is not in their destiny to be together in life.

If there is no difference between us
Then why this silence of gloom between us?

God is that realisation like soul within us
Despite omnipresent, not visible to the eyes

Mistake was equally of both us
You wanted to part, I allowed you to part

Why to blame autumn for gloom in my life
Being flower; withering is in flower's destiny

Ho friend! Do not ask my first wish
You are my first and last wish

People say I laugh a lot
In fact, I am tired of hiding my hurts.

Conscience dies when feelings die
Such death dies an unknown death

A poor for stealing a bread was declared a thief
Politicians despite looting the country remain law makers!!

By Mamutty chola

TONGUE IS TENDER BUT FEW CAN HANDLE

However long the poor may cry, their tears
never get dried up. The poor are very rich in tears
Like an ever green stream

My love, the whole world is in love with you
My love but you are my whole world

Why should I blame you for my misfortune?
It is not your fault, fault is mine ;love happens

Anger is like match box, it burns
self-first before burning others

Those who carry fire of revenge within
Always carry an incurable ulcer within

A life lived with dignity is products of four qualities
They are character, courteous behaviour, noble thought
And respectable and civilized company

Our tongue is very tender and light
But in life, very few people could handle it with care.
By Mamutty chola

Success Is A Journey

Relation in love is like a floating clouds
After short sojourn together flew away like floating clouds

Life's journey is like flow of the rivers
Never stops like a burning candle till dawn

Unaware the waves are, their death is hidden in their success!
They remain protected so long as in the lap of the sea

If you live in the memory of your love like a prisoner
Beware you will be left alone in the journey of life

It is wrong to presume success is final destination
In this fast changing world, all successes are like transit camps

Every evening walk I would see
A tired sun setting in to rise again

These promises of life long company till death
Are like floating clouds, accept the one who is your destiny.
By Mamutty chola

FOR YEARS

What a change!! Now statues are grateful to men
Men can turn a statue into God after worshipping

Remember always, every fame is like a cloud burst
Still men of ego say world exists for them

This evening of gloom made me wander aimlessly
It appears this furlong is familiar to me for ages

Many hopes blossom on your kind gesture
Will any one sets the caged bird free to its freedom?

Gone is gone, don't lament, gone time never returns
But season will come again with spring unlike gone time

Dream high and fly high like falcon in the sky
Beyond moon and stars in the realm of planets

Ho my life! I set out very often in search of self
This journey of search of self is on for ages
To find self is to find my mission on earth.
By Mamutty chola

Treat Your Wine As Your Beloved

How I wished time gone by would have returned like season
We had never been separated with our loved ones in life

Distance is not the reason for the gap in our understanding
Lack of Fidelity and trust are the reasons for the gap between us

Ho life, never takes away my memories
Now my memories are my companion in life

Tried many a time to forget you
Each time I failed since you are my life

It will not make any difference if you depart
Many before came and left show is still on

What a strange link between your thought and my eyes
Whenever your thought comes it brings along tears in my eyes

If you really want to enjoy your wine with all its grace and serenity
Treat your wine as you would love to treat your beloved

Love and peace of mind are like two sides of a river
Have you ever heard meeting of two side of river?

A day would come you would miss me when I am gone
Then you would realise what it had been being together.
By Mamutty chola

BUDS GO WITHER

The lesson that life gives; my friend
I have never found in any book of wisdom

Whenever someone close to me say
Don't worry he is there, I feel I am not alone

Frustrations are those unrealised dreams in life
Like flower buds go whither before blossoming

Yes, it is true life does not cease to exist if loved ones did part
Life goes on but there remains an abyss and vacuum in life

Oh my love; it was you and you only who could feel my feelings
I do try to keep smiling as promised, with a tsunami within me

I derive immense satisfaction by losing to loved ones
Only when the winner is my loved ones, not otherwise

For my emotional momentary decision in life; in retrospect
I regret to no end but now of no use; now atoning for since long

Often I set out all alone on unknown path hoping to meet you
All in vain, since season does come back but not time gone by

One whom I had met years ago, was like my dream realised in life
Alas she was not destined to be mine, we parted like time gone by.
By Mamutty chola

Truth Is Always Lonely

Truth is always bitter for that reason always alone
Falsehood always busy in celebration like thunders

When no one is perfect in life then why
this insistence, all should be perfect in life?

Time is that earth quake under which, not only human
But their unrealized dreams lie buried deep down

Before your breakup think once again, leaving all
She came with you to be with you rest of her life till death
Think of that moments of bliss also spent together

It has been long since destiny parted us apart
But I still see her deep down in my heart's screen

I love darkness of the night because but for darkness
How could we enjoy the beauty of moon, stars and galaxy

I am tired of talking to my loneliness in solitude
Even my memories have become faded and dim

The dry leafs of Autumn give us message, change is life
Don't feel sad for them, they would come again in spring .
By Mamutty chola

Tears Are Language Of Silence

Never break mirror for your ugly look
Ho man, mirror's **existence is truth and truth only**

Secret of my sadness; couldn't wipe out tears of innocents
Still I did care for oppressed whenever opportunity came

I am afraid and I am not answerable to people in the world
When final decision rests with Almighty on the day of judgement

This tantrum of yours you would leave me, think twice
Life's relationships are like gardening; rests on give and take

If you could restrain your emotional outbursts, even for a second
Believe me, you can avert avoidable tragedies in life journey

Tears are language of silence but
Tears of the poor; language of helplessness

Sea thinks sea drops owe their existence to her
Not knowing, the very existence of sea is within the drop

You despite being mine, you never extended your hands
I have seen strangers saving unknown souls from being drawn!!
By Mamutty chola

EMEREGENCE OF INDIA OF OURS

Our recorded history is saga of thousands of years.
People and invaders kept coming down the ages

Mainly Aryan, Afghan, Turk, Uzbek and Mughal
Alexzander, Changes Khan, Nadir Shah, and British

Then question does arise who are the real Indians
As per the renown historians Dravidians are original Indians

Mohenja Daro Harappa civilization proves the points
Then why this noise in the country who is original Indians

Those who came as invaders and rulers adopted this country as theirs
Therefore India is confluence of various cultures, religions and languages

Its shape and geographical reach kept changing based on the the ruler's power
India as country was great during Mourya, Ashoka, and Mughal era

17 century India was called the golden period of India as per European historians. This was the Mughal era of Jahangir and Shah Jahan as reflected in growth and prosperity.

Modern India took birth on 15th August, 1947 after we got liberation from Colonial rules. Even during British era, India had many princely provinces numbering more than 400 in all

AFTER 1947, these princely provinces were merged into liberated India Delhi as capital of India has had seen many regime changes of various dynasties India has survived many ups and downs down, the ages with its unique character of unity in diversity till it emerged as united India of today.

The current turmoils of intolerance is a passing phase since India's resilience to overcome the era of instability and upheavals are well known

Need of the hours is adherence to the values as enshrined in our constitution
The talk of patriotism and nationalism must be inclusive; key to India's survival as nation.
By Mamutty chola

MUSIC IS THE LANGUAGE OF SOUL

Those in power must not supress dissent.
Must have not only the passion but also
patience to listen to the truth

Youth power is the gifted period of life, if channelized,
Impossible can be achieved for humanity

Don't reject suggestions of others in arrogance
Ideas are hidden treasures in the womb of time

The lush green meadow welcomes dewdrops
With smiles and await the arrival of long separated
souls to join to enjoy the bliss filled moments of lives

When I watch evening setting sun with all its glory
Welcoming the dawn of darkness, I await eagerly
For moon, stars and planets in the majestic galaxy

Beauty is truth, truth is god, love is beauty
True love is immortal like time and eternity

Music is language of soul in ecstasy,
Universe is filled with music, be it wind
Sea waves, floating clouds, cool breeze,
Romantic rains, beloved's tender smiles
Dancing peacock or deer in the forest

Or Joyce birds returning to their nests
Or ice covered mountain range, crystal streams

Live in today with joy, today is reality rest; all dreams
Our lives are transitory, but world will go on till eternity.
By Mamutty chola

Made For Each Other

Oh men! you are reflection of universe
Look within to fathom meaning of life
You are the best creation of all creations!

The sculptor carves his love out of stone
Be a sculptor thyself, liberate your love hidden in rocks

Oh soul why do say my body is a prison
When I have given you shelter for life
Why can't we live in peace together?
While together during this sojourn

Oh Moon, oh stars, oh sky we men live to admire your
Eternal beauty. come to think of, but for us, your adoring
Charms would have remained unsung and gone without praise!

Oh saint don't defame wine. she is the truth
If you are with her, you would always speak truth.!

Oh men woman is your mirror, don't break her
You would never realise your worth without her!

Don't you know Adam's life was incomplete without Eve
Even in paradise. You both are made for each other.

Mamutty chola

SMILE IS POWERFUL THAN WORDS

Caution in life is **necessary but too much caution**
will leave you behind being indecisive in life
Hamlet was personification of indecisiveness

To share love means real living
what is there in life without being loved

It is foolish to die for one's believes
When nothing is permanent except change

I am neither an agnostic nor atheist but
I am a theist because there exists invisible power
Beyond human comprehension like soul in our body

One of the symptoms of a psychopath is
their trust deficit in others and insatiable desire
for power such people are narcissists as well
Such people if come to power, nation has to be on guard

Beware! unexpressed or suppressed feelings are
Like dormant volcanoes within us

Love at first sight is a hidden divine spark within us
For one whom we dream in our subconscious mind
For that reason, we say love happens

Music like tears are our eternal companion
In life since birth to death like soul within us

Magic Of Love Is Infinite

It is said that civilization began first time when man
cast word instead of stone. Wrong!!It was not word but smile
Because smile unites being language of peace.
Man is the only creature who carries poison
in his words and love in smile !!

By Mamutty chola

LOVE - THE ESSENCE OF LIFE

You don't become old because of aging.
You become old because of your negative
feelings, thoughts and action in life

Trust me, have faith in self.
If you conquer your fear,
you can win every battle in life

Be adaptable like water
With changing time, don't
be like a stone remain fixed
in time and immune to change

Lessons learned in life; hate divides
Love unites but both are blind!!

Anger is like match stick
Burn self-first before burning others

To err is human. Never be afraid of making
mistakes. Nothing ventures, nothing gains

Excellence is like love.
Perfection is like dream
to live together with love,
A never ending pursuit in life
The very essence and mission in life
By mamutty chola

Our Lives Are Transient Like Sparks

Of all the books ever written by men the book of love is invincible and everlasting, It contains wisdom based on human civilization, If you want to live in peace follow book of love. It is for all time and for all humanity on mother earth.

Do you know moon has black spots on her chest, She been taking all hurts to her heart still spreading love. She is symbol of love, inspiration for nations, poets and lovers. She resides in our hearts being miles away. The full moon light is blessing for mother earth, she shares her beauty and light with all, despite her light being borrowed from sun!

Youth is the best period of life, full of fun, hopes, determination to conquer frontiers for humanity. youth, once gone never comes back unlike old age; once comes never leaves. Our lives are like bubbles, transient and passing.
We men are like passenger on transit ship called time.
No one is perfect except nature—we call god.

Do you know sea is nothing but sea drops. Earth we come from and earth we go to. The mother earth is like an inn for us. This journey of ours is a never ending till eternity. Remember, no one is indispensable.
Our lives are like sparks; very transient
Mamutty chola

BEAUTY LIES WITHIN US

Oh my friend, when I said I love my life most, you felt
Angry and went away without knowing you were my life

When she looked into mirror, wonder struck was the mirror
Seeing the matchless beauty of her, never seen before

Their long awaited togetherness was an occasion for the nature to
rejoice; be it morning breeze, dew's tears of joy

There was music all around; meadows were dancing in bliss.
True love has no barrier being rooted in souls.

The trees are poetry on earth. Still men cut them ruthlessly and
make papers to write saga of nature's destruction by the greed of men,

We men are passengers on transit ship called time, never stops
.Always on move to unknown destination; the biggest mystery of
our lives

The beauty of any thing is rooted in our feelings and not in the eyes
of the beholders!! The real beauty lies within us and not in the
object we look at.
By Mamutty chola

Uderstand True Love

I wonder at times why people betray their love
Like gone time forgetting the one who treated you as his destiny

Now left all alone waiting for lost love, never thought of any
One but you.
All these talks of love till death do us part now sound hallow and
Empty and nothing but betrayal

Without loyalty, fidelity and sacrifice no love can be true love,
True love is rooted in soul and not in external beauty.
In true love lovers live in each other soul. Death can't
separate them. like the love of Laila Majnu, sheree farhad and
Romeo Juliet

Love infatuated with outward beauty is not love but lust.
Such love is transient like floating clouds, melting ice and
autumn leaves

There is no substitute to true love which is eternal like moon,
stars and planets on the galaxy, like morning breeze
ever green meadows, majestic sea waves
Love is unconditional giving, sacrifice and submerging self into
each other soul.

Our universe will last till it moves on the axis of eternal love.
By Mmautty chola

Poetry, Nature's Language

All pains of struggles would turn into smiles
When years' sacrifice turns into success in life

Given the tsunami of changes taking place in our lives
to succeed, one's reach must exceed one's grasp in life.

The phase of changes is so fast one has to be on move
all the time lest one is left behind in life race.

Remember gain is gain, however small it might be.
Sea is the sum total of all the sea drops!

In every culture the metaphor of autumn is used to
express the feelings of desolate and left alone in life
but Autumn is also the harbinger of spring in life!

All religious scriptures were revealed in poetic expression
Which shows God is a perfect poet. Poetry is the language
of the nature.

Love starts and end at motherhood. No other example
worth mentioning in the entire universe. Think of those unfortunate
Souls without mother's love who live with a vacuum and abyss in life.

If love is taken away from the world the whole of the world will turn
into graveyard. No creation on earth can live without love.

By Mamutty chola

Silence 'S Song Is Voiceless

Being listened to and heard is
an eternal human desire
Those who learn to listen
will be darling; be at home,
work place or among friends in society.

If you become a loving person in your feelings,
thoughts, actions or talks, believe me you will
have plenty of friends in your life.
Givers are always gainers

If your approach in life is to be
kind to others rather be right
Your goodwill will soar and you
find you are right in your decision
If not every time but definitely most of the time

As long as you think more is better
you will never be satisfied
This urge to reach and excel
will keep you ahead of others in life

Neither pleasure, nor happiness nor
sadness or gloom are permanent
Things change as time changes.
The beauty of time is it never lasts but
Tough people do.

Attitude matters. If problem is viewed
as hurdle nothing will change but if
Problem is viewed as challenge, every
thing will change including your reach and grasp!!

When silence speaks or sings no one but you can hear.
Silence is the best friend of loneliness.
By Mamutty chola

What Is Beauty

Beauty is a child's smile, Peace is beauty of time.
Parental love is beauty. Also trump of justice over
injustice is beauty.

Beauty is supreme, can take life and give life
Real beauty is rooted in soul; inner beauty

Beauty of dreams have no parallel.
It takes you beyond horizon in the land of
bliss amidst evergreen meadows of solitude

Solitude adds beauty to life,
All the great inventions are gift
of solitude

Separated souls walk in the beauty
of solitude in search of lost love.

Inner beauty is matchless; queen of all beauties
No words can describe elegance and charm of
Inner beauty

Beautiful path has no destination; like
time always on move, an eternal journey
till eternity.

By Mamutty chola

THAT INNOCENT LOOK

That innocent look of my love is still
Fresh in my memory despite lapse of time
Many seasons came and went but my wait
For her is forever till eternity.

Even nature feels for me; be it a morning
Breeze or dew, all are in awe for my sincerity

Her smiles remind me of blossoming of flower buds
The dark floating clouds in the sky remind me of her

Enchanting long black hair, her eyes like serene lake
Her majestic walk reminds me of dancing deer

Her innocence talks of togetherness in future
In retrospect sound like dream of by gone era

Her beauty was matchless like fairy from paradise
She was angel with sublime qualities of grace and love

She would remain deep down in the valley of my heart
Like beckon of light inspiring me to live on with smile

She made me realize what it meant to be in love
and being loved with total dedication, and surrender

It has been ages since destiny took her away from me
But her thoughts will always be part of my life till eternity.

By Mamutty chola

IMMORTAL BOND WITH BELOVED

I am grateful to god for giving
me a companion like you, my love

In every birth after births you only
and you only have been my love

I have felt you in all nature's creations in every form
Be it flower. Moon light, morning breeze

Be it sea waves, floating clouds in the sky
In the echo of temples and churches bells
Be it Aazan from mosques or guru wani
from gurudwara

Be it the melodies of the boats men, musical
Flow of rivers and streams, or the dancing crops
Across the green field spread miles and miles

The ice covered mountains kissing the sky
The birds and falcon flying in the sky
The majestic trees and its dancing branches
I found you my love in every spark of nature

These bond of togetherness will remain till eternity
Messages of praise keep pouring from heavens
Not only angels even nature is awe at our love for each other

Now I am convinced our souls will remain together
Not in this life but in every life till eternity; being infinite!!!
By mamutty chola

PROMISES LIKE FLOATING CLOUDS

If spring happens to knock at my door, after I have gone
tell her I have since settled down in vast desert away
from human civilization.

It is wrong to presume all smiling faces are mirror
of happiness. Each person carries a storm within.

How can I forget those tear-filled eyes of my love,
while parting for good? Those sad look still haunts
me despite ages since gone by.

Those sad souls, and silent faces moving in the crowd
Carry a hidden tsunami within, yearning for a place
Under the sun since ages hoping against hopes.

The never ending sadness, melancholy, loneliness
and deprivation are the gift of my love who came
like a spring in my life but left behind a never ending
Autumn, emptiness, vacuum and abysses in my life.

The promises of life together till death did part us
were like shallow and floating clouds without shade and rain
By Mamutty chola

Who Cares?

Strangers meet and fall in love
Make promises to be together
Till death does them part.

But when comes trial of love. All
Promises become like writings on sand
Or floating clouds; go with the winds
Leaving behind autumn's gloom.

What to talk of human even birds?
Migrate from withered trees to green tree
To make their nests.

Why to blame the world.
When it is the ways of the world.
Who cares when self-interest is supreme
Everything is an option and not an obligation.

I did receive a letter from her
when opened found it blank

Of course there were few tears drops
which explained her helplessness

Did write a letter in reply but
couldn't post, when opened today
after years found the ink still wet!!!

By Mamutty chola

SMILE A FREE INVESTMENT IN GOODWILL

Try to live under the glow of your excellence
Never live on borrowed image. Must know
the difference between fake and original.

Get inspired by roles models but evolve
your personality based on your
own capabilities and attributes.

Those who fall again and again and rise again
And again will be an inspiration for others.

Negativity is the mother of all evils.
Transform your negativity into gravity as magnet
to attract people as friends in your life.

Fill the world with beautiful smiles
Which is a free investment in your good will!!
By Mamutty Chola

My Heart Is Restless Today

My heart is very restless
Don't know the reason, why?

Many phases of life came and went
But never got peace at heart

Take heart, don't get disappointed
This bad phase of life is transient

Your sufferings are results of your actions
Keep faith in God and believe in self

God is benevolent, merciful and kind
Everyone has to live his sojourn on earth

Time is supreme, no one can defy destiny
Nothing ventures, nothing gains is a truth

This is a cardinal principles of nature
Givers are always gainers; trust me

We have come from earth go back to earth
Soul is immortal then why to worry

Keep your thought pure
Truth is God and infinite

Believe me, God nether lives in statue nor in Kashi
God always resides within you and in your feelings,

World exists for you, you don't exist for the world
Like sea is within the seadrop and not other way around

Bad time will not last but tough people do last
Don't you know there is no night without a day
By Mamutty chola

Came Like A Fairy

When you are with me time flies
But when you are away,
even a day sounds like ages.

Oh my love, what a delight to hear
I am your first and last love.

True love is like innocent children's love
Who fight and make up by hugging each other.

I love to be lost in your love forever
Just as I have regained my love forever.

However long I spend time with you
Still I feel you have just come.

My love, your smile is an invitation
To life again again to be together for ever.

When I had met you for the first time
I knew you would be my love for ever.

You came into my life like fairy from heaven.
But went away like floating clouds beyond horizon
Never to return. I wait in gloom with abyss and vacuum
In life.
By Mamutty chola

YOU ARE MY LOVE, MY LOVE

You are my life, my aspiration and my smile
And will remain today, tomorrow and forever

I declare to the whole world I only love you
And will continue to love you
Even after death; if there is life !!!

You can't imagine what you mean to me
All these beautiful scenery have
No attraction for me without you

Oh my love, you are my first and last love
You are my life and I have longed nothing
But you. Your smile radiates my life like rainbow

He was deprived of love for ages like blind
When looked at her enchanting beauty,
Regained his lost vision and exclaimed!
Why he was searching his love in darkness

Even if fate does us part
My love you will ever remain in the
Deep depth valley of my heart for ever.

By Mamutty chola

My Destiny

Oh my friend, you have a right to judge me
Provided you yourself is perfect

Yes, my love, you are always in my thought
Whether it is morning or evening

But it is also true, you are
Not the same love, you have since changed

The hurt of your going away
Lives within me like an ulcer

Those promises of love together
Were like fog ;went with floating clouds

We met with smile but
Departed with hurt in life

Destiny did us part, still
My eyes look for you wherever I go

Whenever you are alone
Do think of our days together
The best period of my life

Our chanced meeting years ago
And our parting of ways to land of unknown
In retrospect, I feel why to blame   you or the world
When you were not destined to be mine.

By Mamutty chola

FRIENDSHIP IN LOVE

The bond of love is stronger in tragedy
than in happiness; love being rooted in heart and soul

Peace at heart, mental tranquillity, serenity of soul
Dominate and flourish when love reigns supreme.

Live your life in such way your heart yearns for
the company of your loved ones together always and ever

Love knits together two strangers's heart
Till death do them part, the magic of love

Beauty of death is that it always reminds us
the good qualities of the departed soul.

The bond of love is stronger in tragedy
than in any other relationships.
For that reason, we say
love gives life and hate takes live.

If there are no friendships between loved ones,
Such relationships may not last.Because friendship
Emphasis is on equal treatment and love demands
unconditional surrender!! The main reasons for break ups
of modern day love marriages world over!!!.
By Mamutty chola

IT BEEN YEARS SINCE WE PARTED

My love it has been years since we parted
But you still remain part of me despite lapse of time

The more I try to forget the more your thought comes
All attempts failed. You are always part of me and shall remain

You and you are only my love in this life and hereafter
You reside deep depth in my heart like my heart beats

How can I forget those beautiful days spent together?
It was like yesterday; gone time never comes back but memory does

Your love for me was unmatched and exceptional
We lived like one soul in two bodies like a fairy from heaven,

Very thought of yours reminds me of those bliss filled days
Spent together talking of life together unaware of cruel destiny

Yes my love, your loss is irreparable, I live with an abyss and vacuum
We are separated by act of destiny but you are within me

Those memories of the days spent together shall remain
Ever green in the deep valley of my heart away from the
gaze of cruel world

Deep down from the depth of my soul, I wish you all the
happiness with your loved ones who are now your world
By Mmautty chola

What Is Your Relations With?

Loneliness and memory
Silence and patience
Meeting and separation
Arrogance and humility
Fame and ill-known
Tears and smile
Friendship and enmity
Love and hate
Happiness and sorrow
Night and day
Rich and poor
Life and death
Spring and Autumn
Flower and thorn
Kindness and cruelty
Progress and backwardness
Victory and defeat
Youth and old age
Rise and   downfall
Closeness and aloofness
If you think you could realize
How precious life is
Live every moment with joy
Which is key to success
All these are nothing but
Two aspects of our lives
Which gives you message
How to live and spend
your sojourn on earth
By Mamutty chola

GIFTS OF NATURE

Memories of youth are eternal companion of life
First love is everlasting and remain fixed in mind's screen for ever
My love's beauty is matchless like fairy from heaven, what moon, what stars and what galaxy all are in awe of my love's beauty

In full moonlit night sea tides rise like mountain, waves struggling to cross the shore, not knowing they would cease to exist Their safety is within in lap of sea. Waves are eternal friends of humanity,
Been inspiring us to keep the struggles on in life since time immemorial

When I go for walk, I walk on lush green meadows covered with dew I enjoy the majestic dawn with sun rising from east. Morning breeze touching my cheek Leaves on the trees dancing in ecstasy with blow of morning soothing wind.
Advent of spring brings greenery all around. Trees are dressed up like brides

Birds flying in grove in search of food leaving the kits in nests on top of the trees. Away from wicked eyes of eagles and snakes. Green fields spread miles and miles, ice covered mountain kissing the sky, far off boat men singing melodies are a thing of beauty all around, indeed gifts of nature to humanity.
Nature is indeed benevolent and kind for ever.
By Mamutty chola

WHEN I SIT BACK AND REFLECT---

When I sit back and reflect on the time gone by,
When I sit back and reflect on the love I got and lost,
When I sit back and reflect on the beautiful days together with my love,
When I sit back and reflect on the struggles I have been through Like sea waves
which keep inspiring humanity from time immemorial,
When I sit back and reflect on my friends from school, college and work place,
When I sit back and reflect on the loss of loved ones and their departure to kingdom of unknown -heavenly abode,
When I sit back and reflect on the lives of the teeming millions struggling for two times meals,
When I sit back and reflect on slum children who grow up without experiencing thrills of childhood!!
When I sit back and reflect on youth and time; once gone never come back unlike season,
When I sit back and reflect on success everything is transient,
Realisation dawn on me everything in life is transient like bubbles on the water except change,

So struggles are on and will remain on ;change being permanent; till eternity.
By Mamutty chola

SEPARATED NEVER MEET

Yes, love is eternal, true love never dies
Remains ever youthful; soul being immortal.

Years have gone by since destiny did us part
Never for a moment I could forget you, my love.

The days down the years, many seasons came
But you never came, my wait still on.

While parting you took a promise I must keep my smile
Yes, I do smile with abyss and vacuum within in my life.

I am still under the spell of your beauty, and grace
You were centre of my life .Could't take away a glance
From your hyponastic eyes reminding me of serene lake,

Time spent in each other's arms away from the cruel
gaze of the world are the treasures of my life
Years ago while in college when we first met.
At your first smile, said my soul you are mine.

Now I have lost all hopes of ever meeting you in life.
I do not know where are you and how are you.?

I always wanted best for you. So wish all the happiness
On earth with your loved ones who are now your world.
Keep smiling as ever; my lost love .

Your memory is that invaluable gift
It's always better to have loved and lost
Then never to have loved at all.

Life without love is like a barren land
Vast and dissolute like an empty desert.
By Mamutty chola

YOU ARE MY LOVE

Ever since you came in my life
I always wait for you. day and night
I wish to be with you together
in your arms, under the gaze of full moon
night and radiant stars above in the sky
You my love, rejuvenated my dormant life
And made me feel I am worth loving, beautiful.
adorable and can fall in love.
You appeared as rainbow in my dark sky
With all your charm, beauty and glow
Now I declare to the world, I am in love
With you and you only, my love.
You are the prince charming of my dream
And you are my first and last love.
You my love; only made me feel what
it means to be in love and being loved.
Thank you my love for your unconditional love.
Now I know love means caring and giving.
By Mamutty chola

MAGIC OF SELF ADMIRATION

Oh God ever since I decided to love my own self
I experienced great transformation within me

I was unaware, never concerned and never thought
How lonely had been my soul without me

I was searching in vain happiness outside
Forgetting my own happiness lies within me

There is a need to know the aspiration of your soul
To know yourself to strive for happiness in life

Those who are in love with themselves
Are seen loving the world with joy and passion

I suggest when you get up in the morning look at
Your reflection in the mirror and admire yourself

Your sad life will transform into
Happy life with magical effect

Never neglect your soul and make
your body a prison for your soul

Your biggest asset of your life
Is you and you only my friend

Remember, world exists for you,
Never, you exist for the world

Like a sea drop is not mere drop,
The whole of sea exists within the drop!!!
By Mamutty chola

Me And My Memories

Early morning when I looked outside through window
Spring was in full bloom, all the trees were
Dressed up with fresh leaves and flowers like brides

The leaves were dancing with the gentle flow of
morning breeze. To cap it all, birds were singing
in praise of nature for the gift of spring boom

I couldn't't resist thinking of our days together
Your memories came rushing like action replay
All efforts to forget in vain, you are part of me

When we met, thought my dreams realised
But cruel hands of destiny took you away from me
I never loved you because of your exceptional beauty

Not because of your hypnotic eyes resembling serene lake
Not because your enchanting long hair like floating dark clouds
Not because of your rosy cheek and lips like rose petals

Not because of your beauty like fairy from paradise
Not because of your majestic walk like peacock and deer
Only and only because you loved me for my sake
Your love for me was exceptional and unconditional

Your memories have been my co-travellers in life
When alone I look at moon and see your reflection
Never ask how I have spent days which were impossible to spend
Be happy with your loved ones who are your destiny and life now
ByMamutty chola .

My Journey Of Loneliness

How I wished I had the company of my lost love
In the journey of life. That would have turned
The journey into bliss like;
Morning cool breeze
Enchanting moonlit night
Advent of spring
Musical flow of crystal streams
Birds singing in wait for their mates
Rainbow in the dark clouds loaded with rain
Walking on bare feet on morning dew

Alas! mine had been journey of loneliness since long
At times, I console self-let bygone be bygone

Why to lament in vain rest of life. Change would
come like changing season, not like gone time!!

I would go on walking absent minded lost in
Thought in search of self
Truth is this sojourn of mine on earth has been like forlorn
In the vast desert amidst changing dunes at the mercy of
Velocity of the wind

My life has seen nothing but struggles all along
Like a boat caught up in tempest since long.
By Mamutty chola

LESSON OF LOYALTY

Early morning when I look out through my bedroom windows
The scenic beauty with the arrival of spring is beyond description

Lush green trees spread miles and miles dressed up like brides
To cap it all, birds of various species are welcoming the spring

With their melodious songs amidst cool morning breeze
All birds live in harmony unlike we human beings

We being humans never learned anything from nature
Though birds too are selfish, they never make their nests
On withered trees!!

Whether animals or birds all live with their own folks
And never kill each other from their own clans

Unlike animal, we humans, kill fellow human for our selfish ends
Even snake does not bite unless provoked or threatened

Human civilization is nothing but saga of atrocities, wars, genocide
We being homo sapiens, intolerance is in our genes!!!

Dogs and horse despite being unable to communicate the way men do
They are the finest examples of loyalty and love, men must emulate

Ours I, me and myself approach are reasons for trust deficit among us
For that reasons, even amidst million crowd men find themselves lonely

Ho men , if we had learned lesson of loyalty from animals
Our world would have been a cradle of peace and love.
By Mamutty chola

LESSON FROM DEATH

For nothing death is ill-known and despised
I say death is matchless in her commitment

Her love is unparalleled and unmatched
Never blame death for being ungrateful

Is there any example in human history?
When death had ever failed in her duty

We human suffer untold miseries while alive
Still we adore, love and admire life till death

Death for performance of divine duty
She is feared, dreaded, despised and avoided

We, men knowing death is definite still curse death!!
What a hypocrisy, death being certain, still we blame death.
By Mamutty chola

OH! MY LIFE

Morning comes, evening comes
But life goes on non stop as routine

Hopes do emerge from the womb of dreams
Alas, when my eyes open find self in loneliness

How I wished I had the company of my love
Life would have been cradle of joy and bliss

I been in search of lost love for years but in vain
Life was only joy, bliss and smiles when together

Will there be any end to the endless loneliness of mine?
Ho my life tells me what to do, there is darkness all around

My memories of time spent together getting dimmed
How can I pass the sojourn on earth without memories ?
By Mamutty chola

Autumn Amidst Spring

Let the fanatics destroy temple, mosque, and church I do not care
Let them not for God sake break people hearts where love resides

The dark clouds in the sky are signs of impending storms waiting
To engulf. I am worried, ho God, where the innocent birds would spend their night.

It been years we parted company, why to lament lost love
Whom I loved with all passion, but she was not destined to be mine

The abyss, the vacuum and the emptiness are my destiny
I am like a lone traveler in vast desert amidst dunes at the mercy of storms

Ho my love; I did pretend not to know you
Lest you become subject of discourse among friends.

Despite being with loved ones, he always felt lonely
Reason; absence of love and care for his sake

Last night I had a dream, amidst spring
It was autumn every where. What does it mean?

By Mamutty chola

Never Wait For Gone Time

I have neither proof nor any argument but I have faith
Ho God, your name is so brief but your description
beyond description.

If possible, spend time with smile
who does not have shadow of gloom in life.

I am not a merchant of dreams unlike others.
Always speak truth; journey of truth is always lonely.

After a long wait today my life asked me where
Is that person for whom I waited all my life
I confessed to my life, it was my mistake to wait for
Gone time!

Your hurt would increase manifold, if you know
The person hurting you is none other than your loved one.

How I wished if I had a beloved one
Who could read my tears in rain.
By Mamutty chola

SONGS OF MEMORY

This beautiful scene of sunrise in east
The caravan of dark floating clouds in the sky
Bring along music of love of my love
The dark clouds neither bring rain nor storm
Only shade of floating clouds with its romance
Learn to live every moment of life with smile
Time gone, youth gone never return unlike season
Separated souls in love do unite either in this life
Else in the God's kingdom   since soul is immortal
Hear the cry of hungry in million on mother's earth
They yearn for two times meals nothing else
Rising gap between rich and poor world over
Not only disturbing but alarming as well
Never build your dream house on poor's land
Beware of God's fury and   justice.
Many tyrants came and went unsung
Now resting in their unknown graves
Tolerance of injustice is oppression
Ho men; an invitation to revolution.
Solution lies in empathy, love and care
Love unites, hate divides say all scriptures.
By Mamutty chola

YOUR ARE MATCHLESS, MY LOVE

I admit my mistakes with regrets
For becoming victim of suspicion
My love Left me years ago
I still wait for her in repentance
When friends ask what is love
I just smiled, think of my love
Distance does create misunderstanding
World get chance for conspiracy
Ho my love, how can I burn your letters
They are not mere letters, gift of love
When I glance at words of those letters
I feel your presence in my soul
When alone I do visit those beautiful meadows
Where we spent walking arms in arms together
I may meet many in life in sojourn while alive
But none like you, yes, my love while alive
Days went, years went but my wait still is on
With cherished hopes to reunite with love.
By Mamutty chola

On Time Canvas

Question is not what you are?
Question is whether you are truthful in life
Take every step with caution and foresight
The best course to ensure success
Unity is strength
Disunity is recipe for failure
When unity and diversity unite
End results will be excellence and matchless
Time gone is history
Today is the creator of your future
Ho men , don't leave anything for tomorrow
Tomorrow never comes, today is the reality
Yesterday is dead and tomorrow is like fog
Live in today, your future is hidden in today
Every day is good day provided
Your intents are good so act now.
Action is life, inaction is death
Remember my friend; time and youth
Once gone never come back
Become a painter of eternity
Leave on time canvas your mark till eternity,
Like the portrait of Mona Lisa by Leonardo da Vinci
By Mamutty chola

THERE WAS A TIME

I was on top of fame
I am now nobody but my shadow
Ignorance is curse
Soul is starved to death
Education is not only a refuge
But enrichment for soul
It is wrong to think you can change future
Create capabilities within you
Let there be demand for your
Talent everywhere like magnet
Whoever controls situation
Controls direction of his life
Time passes, situation changes
Circumstances are co-travelers of time
Guide you to your destination in life
The lesson I have learned in life
Change being permanent
All success is like a transit camp
So every step is an examination in life!!
By Mamutty chola

In Praise Of Moon

Despite hurts of ages in heart, Moon shares its light
With all, though borrowed from sun
Moon is the reason for joy and smile for all
So Moon resides in very one's heart as darling
Despite being miles and miles away still so near
Moon is symbol of love, beauty and elegance
Moon is the harbinger of new year, and festivals
Moon occupies pride of place on national
Flags of many countries around the world
Moon's beauty, and charms is unparalleled.
Full moon is the inspiration for poets, and lovers
Moon enhances the beauty of Taj Mahal
Lovers from world over flock to TajMahal during full moon
Moonlight is gift of nature to humanity
Moon is the heart beats of lovers of all ages around the world
Lovers see reflection of their beloved on moon
Moon is worried since men has set their feet on Moon
Human being homo sapiens, moon is worried
Men once settled they will divide the moon
On the basis of caste, colour, and religion
And would destroy Moon's beauty and   secular values
As men had done to mother earth for their greed!!!
By Mamutty chola

WITHIN SMALL ACTS OF LOVE ----

*L*ike always small idea is the harbinger of
Major change in life so are little acts of love
Which turn our lives into bliss and joy for all?

Why ho man! why do you spend
your life in loneliness and darkness
Enjoy nature in its lush green
Meadows, this life is like a bubble

Faith is unshakeable like Gibraltar rock
Does shape our character in life

Echo of sad music of humanity you
May hear amidst dark lanes and by lanes
Of human ghettos and slums where
oppressed and forgotten subsist without hopes

As a child we are told God resides above in
The sky in heaven but God is within us
What are these heaven and hell but illusion!!

Flowers lament saying they are destined to live
Among thorns forgetting but for thorns their
Safety is always in danger. what a miracle
Of nature for its creation on earth.

Feelings of sadness, joy, love and deprivation
All live within us as strangers like soul within us.

Humanity world over live simultaneously
Within three strata of society; rich,
middle class and poor with their hopes
Aspirations and frustrations within them
Self-made world of make belief.

Time and circumstances are co-travellers
Both are inseparable; giving rise
To success and failure in life

By Mamutty chola

POETRY OF EARTH IS INFINITE

When we look around amidst nature
We can hear and feel music of earth
Be it wind, rain, sea waves, flow of river
Dancing trees, buds blossoming in the garden,
Birds welcoming the arrival of spring with joy,
Also Sad melody of falling leaves in autumn
So we say poetry of earth is infinite.

Among the most powerful languages, silence,
The most powerful of all. It does convey what it
Wants to convey remaining silent.
So wise says silence is gold!!

The main object of all religions is to make man
The bliss of heaven within him during his sojourn on earth.

Persons with humble background with character when
come to occupy Position of authority, they do transform
the course of human history for betterment of humanity
It has been the saga of human civilization dawn the ages.

The fear if viewed with fear consequences will always be
Negatives. However fear if viewed positively then it is
Mother of foresight!

Resort to immoral means to achieve moral goal
Is unethical. It is like assuring abode to homeless people
In dream homes by politicians to perpetuate themselves in power.

By Mamutty chola

IF LOVE IS RELIGION, WORLD IS PARADISE

If humanity had declared the love as the greatest religion
Our lives would have been a cradle of joy, harmony, care, and sacrifice !!

Do you know that thing which is darling of all, rich, power and deprived?
It has no religion, colour, caste but acts as magnet, it is called money, the real secular identity of the world!!!

We can always find beauty in God's creation be it human, nature, birds, animals provided you see beauty within you.

People in real love merge into one losing their own identity.
Then the question of I, me, you and yourself ceases to exist.
They live as one soul in two bodies.

In the world nothing is real unless it is experienced by us
till then it remains in the realm of unreal.

You have the choice always to choose your friend in life but not an enemy.
Enemies in your life are gift of times and circumstances. Circumstances being the co-travellers of time, you are forced to accept and face the situation.

Heard melodies are experienced, felt and inhaled so become immortal
But excellence has no finishing point. There are million melodies
Hidden in the womb of time awaiting to emerge from behind the horizon.
By Mamutty chola

ALL CREATURES ARE CREATED IN PAIRS

Flight of imagination is unlimited. For that reason,
poets, philosopher and scientists have vision to
fathom the unfathomable in the womb of time.

Dreams give birth to hope
Hope creates future. Thought
and action are means to realise your goal.
So dream you must to excel in life.

No love can last between lovers
if there is no friendship between
them. Reason, love demands unconditional surrender.
Whereas friendship believes in give and take on
equal footing. The genesis of failure of love marriages.

Change being permanent, those who demand conformance
And consistency in the organisation context in all situations
it will be recipe for self-extinction.Because no success is permanent
And all are transient. Case in point is fashion industry.

Man being social animal, can't live alone. Even nature has
Created all creatures; be it human, birds, animals, fish, and
Insects in pairs. For that reason, people in love, if got separated
find soul mate in life. Loneliness is the worst form of suffering
like solitary confinement.
ByMamutty chola

Every Night Has A Dawn

He has been in wait since long for better days to come but all in vain
When he sits and reflects on when did he smile last, he couldn't't
recall
Since it has been years. He very often wonders, why did God
script his destiny with gloom and despair.

He had never thought that his mistakes of the moment; committed
in bliss would turn out be a punishment for life.
One whom he lifted from abject despair and made his companion
in life Turned out be his ACHILLES' HEEL.

His dream home built with care and love remains a deserted abode.
No sign of joy, and song of love. His life journey on his sojourn
on mother earth been a long forlorn.

When in relations, if trust deficit reigns supreme, absence of love
and care creep in; such relations are doomed to failure.

However, his faith and belief in his creator is unshakable like
Gibraltar rock. He knows Autumn is not infinite but harbinger
of spring!!
By Mamutty chola

BELOVED'S WAIT FOR HER LOVE

Oh my love ! my dishevelled hair waiting for your loving touch
My tears filled eyes are waiting to absorb you within me.

My thirsty lips are waiting for your enthralling kisses since long
Your long awaited arrival has made my soul restless since long

Oh my love!, come soon don't keep me waiting endlessly
Remember, I will wait for you till eternity, you mean my life

Without you this life means nothing to me, remember always
Many seasons came and went still waiting since I know you would come.

You are like season, will come not like time which once gone ,
never comes. Morning cool breeze has message for me of your arrival
My gaze is fixed at door hoping you would knock at my door.

This life of mine is your pledge, awaiting your arrival since long
You are my first and last love remember always my love.

Oh my love! do you remember our meeting together on sea shore
Every evening after college and those innocent talks of life together

Even the sea waves are our confidants they too miss you
Oh my love! my love for you is infinite .come soon; waiting for you

Oh my love ! my dishevelled hair waiting for your loving touch
My tears filled eyes are waiting to absorb you within me.

By Mamutty chola

MAGIC OF LOVE

If here is love within you
The whole world looks beautiful.

The beauty of sun, moon, stars
And galaxy will remain unsung.
If we are devoid of love just like
A blind man who is deprived of vision
 To see and admire beauty in its prime

When we are filled with joy, bliss and smiles
It radiates all around like moonshine.

Songs are of many types; of sorrow,
happiness, melancholy, union, separation.
Our souls resonate when we hear melodies
of sad songs

Like day which enables us to enjoy the beauty of nature
Night gives us opportunity to enjoy the beauty of
Moonlight, stars glow and magical solar systems.

Poets like nightingales give their best lyrics
In solitude in memories of their lost loves.

The enthralling kisses of the long separated
lovers when unites ; their souls meet in the
lush green meadows of bliss.

Never feel sad my love,. Autumn is always
The harbinger of spring. Joy and sorrow come
and go like seasons do. Time passes into oblivious
abyss like morning breeze!!
By Mamutty chola

Why Are You Sad At Heart?

Oh God let me not stretch my hands
Before others, as I do before you.

Our memories are like photo album
Which preserve events of the past in
Our mind's screen till our last day

Memories without events are like
Blank papers, nothing more nothing less

Mirror never loses its originality even after
Breaking into several pieces but emerges
In many pieces by retaining its originality.

It been years since I have been feeling sad at heart
When asked came the reply, there is no peace at heart.

Very often I hear, when alone , a screams from
The deep down valley of my heart, it sounds like
Cry of my love in deep sorrow for help.

Oh my friend have you ever seen rejected and rusted clock
Left alone, never lead a life of rusted clock. Life is too precious
to be wasted over the past failures.
By Mamutty chola

CHANCED MEETING WITH MY LOST LOVE

How can I forget my chanced meeting?
With my lost love at airport after years.

When our eyes met we couldn't' believe
My gaze was fixed in disbelieve at her.
Same was her reaction in disbelieve.

I had given up all hopes of ever meeting her.
There was sadness writ large all over her face
An index of time spent in loneliness
She has lost her charm, grace, beauty
Smile, her eyes once centre of beauty were dim
Like withered flowers in the autumn gloom
I was trying to locate my lost love in a stranger

She said life had been like prisoner in the
Prison of gone time memories. She did try
To live in present but all in vain said she with tears .

To her question how had been my life without her
In reply tears rolled down like a stream waiting to burst.

But I was happy true love never dies being immortal
we still live in each other souls like ever before.
Meeting her was like a dream fulfilled in life

Magic Of Love Is Infinite

As she was to avail of her connecting flight
Despite our undying love for each other,
we said goodbye to each other.
I stood lost in her love.saw her disappearing
In crowd once again, never to meet again, we were
Now like two banks of a river never destined to meet ever.
By Mamutty chola

OH MY DARLING LOVE

Meeting with my love after long wait was
Like regaining life. we both lost in each other's
Arms would spend magical ecstatic moments
Hours together unmindful of the world
Around planning for the future together till death do us part.

My love's beauty was unmatched like a fairy from heaven
Her princess like look, sexy lips, glowing cheeks,
intoxicating eyes like serene lake amidst nature.
we were made for each other
But destiny had other plans, I lost her for good

Today Since morning I am feeling very lonely at heart.
Even sun is setting in west tired like an old man for rest

Felt like penning down my pent up feelings for a while
My Words would be my expression of pains, cry of
Depressed, oppressed and deprived souls. Struggling
for two times meals. From my writing will emerge flame.

I find solace and comfort in wine like divine
Not in temple, mosque or church either
Oh pious man, how can I explain the magic of wine unless
You taste it once. It will take you in its wings like falcon
High above the sky in the realm of bliss beyond the horizon
Then you will know the real meaning of life!
By Mamutty chola

Listen To The Cry Of Your Feelings

Do you ever hear the cry of your feelings?
If you have not, then listen to it in your
solitude all by yourself.

Friendship is like love but not complete like
Love.Love demands complete surrender
Whereas friendship is based on equal treatment.

Morning dews are not mere dews but tears of
The nature on the ongoing destruction of mother
Earth by the men in their craze for development.

Fame and fans following are based one sided obsession
The relation is totally transient. One who commands following
Does not know the fans. The fans also forget their role models
Once they lose fame.

Never narrate your tales of woes before others.
Who has time for you when the whole world is
In the grip of crisis.

Whenever I sit down to write I detach
Completely from self so that I can give
A detached account without subjectivity
Because, if you write with attachment
The reality will remain hidden from world
If that be so the purpose of writing is incomplete.
By Mamutty chola

RAIN MAKES ME NOSTALGIC

First rain brings memories of past
The blissful days spent together with
Lost love arms in arms in pouring rain.
She would read my tears of joy in rain.

Rain would enhance her beautiful wet hair
And glowing face like full moon in the night.

The blissful days spent together in rain
Now seems like dream of bygone days.

Fresh rain today made me nostalgic
I set out in rain on the known path
All alone with loving memories of my Lost love.
I went and sat on the seas shore. Waves
we're dashing to cross the shore and touching
My Feet as if they were asking where is my love
And why I have come alone. Waves had been our
Confidants for years. We had spent many blissful
Days together on the sea shore playing with waves.

Nowadays she often comes in my dreams assuring me
If she is still mine and ever be mine. Wants me to take care.

When I sit and reflect, all my wait had been in vain.
I am left alone in life. My loneliness is my perennial
co-traveler. I now love to enjoy my loneliness in solitude
I can't allow my loneliness to suffer since I love my life.
By Mamutty chola

LOVE THE LIFE

I was sitting lost in thought in bygone days
Heard a knock at the door. When opened
Saw my lost love standing at the door. Before me
With her usual touching and caring smile

Could't believe it could happen to me. She stepped in
and hugged me with tear filled eyes.
We remained in each other arms Not believing in my luck
The strains of separation were visible on her face.
No longer looking cheerful since, had lost her youth and grace

But her eyes were same full of love for me with the serenity of
calm lake as ever before. She caught hold of my hand and
said she would always be mine, none can separate us now.

Suddenly I heard the voice of my grandson who was waking
me up. When opened the eyes it was already day break.
Looked outside through windows of my bedroom
Saw the birds on the trees as usual singing and welcoming the
arrival of spring.
Trees were all dressed up with fresh leaves like brides

Thought to self. Season does come but gone time and youth never
come back..
Life goes on. we may come we may go. I have now decided to live
my life in dreams of my grand son's dream,
By Mamutty chola

MY CONCERNS FOR LOVED ONES

Why this gloomy clouds in my life once again today?
Why does the gloom have special love for me in life?

Days went, months sent and years went by
Leaving behind the traces of gloom in my life

Though I love darkness, I enjoy the charms, and beauty
of moon, stars and Galaxy in the night all by myself

But there are other pressing demands concerning'
my loved one's life.I have a commitment to redeem

That I have to restore once again the happiness and
and smiles of my loved ones; lost for my follies

My mistakes of moment cost me every things
In life. Oh God view my lapses with empathy

I want to see my loved ones fully secured against
the vagaries and uncertainties of life, when I am gone

I am at the twilight of my life.Life is so uncertain
not a single second is within my control, hence the prayers.
By Mammuty Chola

Secret Of Happiness

You must have a focused aim in life
All energy directed at that aim in life

Shall always be grateful to creator
For bestowing on you faculty of mind

Learn to love your life while alive
If you are not there, what is the life?

Have faith in today in life
Never waste your today for better tomorrow

Today is what matters, tomorrow is a dream
Have faith in power of time; the omnipotent

The time is power and wealth also
Make use of your time as diamond

Try to act out of the box for excellence
Put your heart and soul whatever you do

Go on adventure to feel the thrills of life
Maintain and lead always a balanced life

Take time out for self and loved ones in life
Maintain working relations with all in life

Be it home, office or social life
Act like gardener for harmony and growth

Never pick up a job or profession in life
Where your heart and soul not happy

Believe in giving rather in taking
Remember, givers are always gainers

Fun and joy are voice of your soul
Share happiness and be happy in life
,
Life means funs, actions and celebrations
Leave a mark in life so you are remembered

Focus in life has to be on what is wrong
Never, ever on who is wrong in life

Never be afraid of making mistakes
To err is human being decedent of Adam and Eve!!!

Finally remember always, your best friend and worst enemy
Are your thoughts and actions so be on guard and think positive
By Mamutty chola

Flight Of Imagination

Very often my aspirations would ask me how long this wait
This question inspires to redouble my efforts to aim high

I have since suffered a lot by trusting others in good faith
Now I am determined to achieve my goal come what may

My pursuits have been on since long like sea waves
I have to redeem promised made to my loved ones

Give back their deprived beautiful smiles to them
They suffered for reasons of my failures and follies

Life has taught me one hard lesson; there is no luck
Everything is got written, if you have the capabilities

I hold none responsible for my miseries and set backs
I alone am responsible for my ups and downs in life

Our best friends and worst enemies are we ourselves
Our thoughts and actions make us what we; never blame destiny

So I dreams and dreams and keep my imagination high above the sky
Like falcon, the new world await us beyond Moon and stars in planets.

By Mamutty chola

SOLITUDE OF MY HEART

Seen in garden flowers and thorns
Live in harmony unlike we human beings

Being human, we live like adversaries and enemies
There always exists trust deficit like two banks of a river

Had a chance to look into mirror after a long gap
Face to face in front of mirror, saw a known stranger

Saw far off hutment set on flame
Asked self why again this destruction

Came message few more hutment set on fire
By forces of darkness, ignorant, intolerant and hatred

What an irony whom I would consider others
Saved my life from communal frenzy and madness

After along gap, I saw the intolerant in the temple
What made him to think of God for atonement

There was light all around except in my house
Thought of giving shelter to darkness for a night!!

The one who was once very close to my heart
When met by chance behaved like a stranger

People often talk of solitude of vast desert
No one knows the solitude of abandoned million.
By Mamutty chola

OH MY BETRAYED LOVE

Was there any need to pretend when
You had made up your mind to desert me?
If you had reposed in me your decision to part
I would have willingly agreed to say goodbye
I am indeed sad on your betrayal since you
Were the one whom I had chosen to be my
Partner in life.
Time is a great healer. It carries within it million
Tragedies of betrayal and broken promises.
I am not the first person in the universe
Who has been betrayed in love. Remember no
One dies of broken heart with the departure
of loved ones either from life or from the world.
But take it from me, my friend, you would miss me a lot
When you happen to meet someone of your nature.
Then you would realise what it would have meant
To be with me or without me in life.
I am indeed lucky I could know your intention
to leave me well on time. Else I would have lived on
in wait for you in vain.
My final message never ever thinks of coming back
Into my life. I will never respond to your call in despair.
Now to live with you again would be like leading a life
Of self-deceit. You be happy in your new world
Let me be happy in my own world.
By Mamutty chola

WHY ARE YOU SAD? OH MOON WHY

Today when I set out for my evening walk
In full moon night. I looked at Moon
She was in her pristine beauty, charm
And glory spreading her moonshine across
the face of earth. Bringing joy and bliss
in the lives of the creatures on earth.

I have often seen image of my lost love
on Moon in full moon. I asked Moon whether
she had seen my lost love any where. Before
Moon could reply, she was engulfed by moving
dark clouds for a few seconds. When she emerged
from the shadow of the clouds, she said no
she had not seen my love anywhere.

I asked her why she had a dark patch on her face.
She replied since ages she had been receiving
Shocks aftershocks on seeing the sufferings
Of the creatures on earth. Her aim had been
to spread happiness all round. .But for
we all, her beauty would have remained unsung
Said the moon.

Moon was very sad for falcon. She said no one had
loved her the way falcon did. He had been flying to
reach her in full moon since ages but alas, all attempts

in vain.No one knew better than her the pangs of separation. Her love for falcon and all others on earth would remain immortal since her soul resides within us; the creatures on mother earth!!!
by Mamutty Chola

IN CONVERSATION WITH MY SOUL

I often indulge in conversation with my soul while alone.
I asked my soul why people have become so self –centred
and selfish. When greed based corruption being the orders of the day
what more you could expect, said my soul with sense of despair.

Soul further explained that since dawn of human civilization
Many revolutions and many regime changes have taken place
But style of governance remained the same, power catered; be
it autocracy, oligarchy, dictatorship, communism, socialism or
democracy. Consequently, poor has become poorer and rich
richer.

The day rulers come to use their authority as responsibility
Our world become a cradle of peace and prosperity; said soul.
But that day will never come in human lives till eternity because
You men are homo sapiens and to dominate and to suppress the weak
Is in your genes and is your USP.

She has now decided on being liberated from body, she would
ask God never send her to any human body to live and suffer a
life of prisoner.

On hearing the soul, I resolved myself to be the creator of my
own destiny. To which my soul echoed and assured me of her
full supportat every steps of my life and be my guest till eternity.
By Mamutty chola

LISTEN TO MIND NOT HEART

We are aware of realities of relationships
Still we are left with no option but to maintain
Them being our destiny,

In life relation with our love is not the
Only obligation in life. There are other relations
Equally important in life to redeem and honour

No one dies in life because of failure in love.
Accepted but, it does make difference in life.

Believe me dawn of realization means life
And life without experience is no life.

Whenever my love calls me with smile
It reminds me of sound of nightingale

In an utter sad mode I happened to go to
Bar to engross self in wine to kill my loneliness
After two sips, my love's Image flashed
Across my mind screen asking me to take care!!

In love separation has been the destiny of all true
Love down the saga of human civilization.
In separation lies the secret of immortality of love
Bearing few exceptions in life. King Edward VIII
.Abdicated his throne for his Love —a commoner

Once my friends wanted to read my hands to
predict my future. I asked them what about
those who don't have hands. Still waiting for a reply!!l

Knowing full well heart is a sentimental fool
Million have suffered listening and acting
as per the dictates of hearts still men ignore
wise counsels of mind down the ages. No
lesson learned in the best tradition of Adam!!!
So we say to err is human.!!
By Mamutty chola

LOVE IS IMMORTAL

Life would have been a cradle of peace, bliss, had she been my companion in life.
But alas, destiny willed it otherwise.
Since her departure life is like a shattered dream for ever.
Now she comes very often in my dreams
And keeps telling me take care, she is always mine..when I open eyes find self-left all alone in life.

I know now I have to be alone in life journey while my sojourn on earth. Destiny sacrificed our love at the altar of religious divide and intolerance.

The time spent with my love now seems a distant dreams of bygone era. Meeting ever with lost love is like gone time which once gone never returns!

She is within my soul.I see and feel her in everything; be it moon.,stars. Cool morning breeze. dancing peacook, deer, majestic waves. serene deep sea. flow of streams. blossomed flowers in the garden, songs of nightingale. Moving caravan of clouds ice filled mountains kissing sky, the dawn, musical rain and lush green meadows.

Separation is hallmark of all true love since down the ages. So why to mourn.
Take lesson from season
Change is permanent. Happiness and sorrow part of life.

Life being a gift, must be lived .
Love unites. inspires and gives strength to live on be it adversity or victory.
By Mamutty chola

Helplesness

My association with Autumn has been since ages.
Life has been under the shadow of darkness since ages

I relish solitude of vast desert; left to serenity of the nature.
When happen to pass by the desolate and deserted garden,

There comes echo of the pains of the thorns similar to my destiny.
Last night devastating storms destroyed totally hundreds of trees.
I am worried where the poor birds will rest tonight oh my God.

My abode has been the resort of darkness for ages. All around
there is light. Thought of giving refuge to darkness for night in
my abode

I was eagerly looking for that tree which would give me and my love
shelter from the scorching heat of summer years ago seems like
by gone era.

After long wait, came a letter from lost love today
When opened found it blank; conveying her helplessness !!
By Mamutty chola

TOGETHER WITH MY LOVE

The happy days spent together with my love are my treasured memories; a source of refuge in loneliness and solitude since the cruel hands of destiny snatched her away to the land unknown; years ago.

Fond memories of my love keeps coming like restless sea waves in turmoil ,non stopped reminding me of blissful days spent together on the sea shore playing with waves.,since lost all hopes of ever meeting her in life. she was matchless in her beauty, charm and grace like a fairy ;all loving and caring like an angel in my life.

I often set out all alone on the known path in search of her footprints but all in vain.My unrealistic hope is still hopeful of finding her.
At times, when alone find self-lost in her arms face covered with her beautiful long hair dancing with cool breeze on the sea shore.

I wish and pray the very best for her. May God keep her cheerful like nightingale in the lush green garden amidst her loved ones. She only taught me what it meant to be in love. She has been a real inspiration in life to live and fight on. Love magic is I indeed infinite, my friends.
By Mamutty Chola

Say Good Bye

It is better to forget we had ever met in life my love. I do not blame you since I know your limitation and compulsion. It has been the destiny of many before us, though made for each other but never destined to be together.
Your love for me is priceless. I set you free from all your promises of life together. But my heart beats for you will never stop till last day of my sojourn on earth.

Your love is and will remain as an eternal flame in my soul and be a source of inspiration to live on. Love being rooted in soul never dies but becomes more enduring and inspiring to live on.

I wish to see you always smiling like blossomed flowers in the gardens Be faithful to one who is going to be your partner in life. He has accepted you knowing your past. Accept him as your destiny. Remember; edifice of love can only be built on trust.

No creature can live alone since nature has made all in pairs. Down the line if I happen to meet someone of your nature make her my partner in life since you are the ultimate finale for me as love goes

Life being gift of nature must be lived; sharing and spreading love. But time spent together will remain ever green deep down in the valley of my heart for ever. Good bye my love.

By Mamutty Chola

ALL ARE SELFISH TO THE CORE

Seen many lovers making promises to be together till death
But experienced; such promises are mere time pass and transient.
When ever happens to meet a better choice in terms of status,
wealth or from the same community.The lovers separate and
migrate like seasonal birds.

What to talk of lovers even birds shift their nests from the withered
trees to lush green trees; selfishness is ingrained. in all   for self-
comfort

In has become a done thing with modern day lovers to change
partners like changing dress.
The era of shire Farhad, wamiq Azra, Soni Mahiwal, Laila Majnu
Romeo Juliet and King Edward VIII, UK who renounced the Throne
to marry his love; Mrs. Simpson a commoner are since long
dead and gone

Better be with one who has chosen you as partner in life lest
you are left alone in twilight of your life. Trust is foundation of
edifice of love.
Remember no one can live alone since nature has created us in
pairs. For that reason rarely any one commits suicide for reasons of
failure in love!!. LIFE IS MENAT TO BE LIVED WITH LOVED
ONES. Past is shadow and dead, Future is like fog. Today is the
reality. In today is hidden your happiness and future!!
By Mamutty Chola

LOVE IS GOD

The whole world is yours if you are in love and being loved
Those who love themselves can only love the world

If you are heartbeat of your loved ones, it gives you immense
strength being wanted. And if you are in love, it inspires you

We are born alone, work alone and die alone.
But through your love and friendship you make
It reality that you are not alone when being loved

Let us always meet others, even if stranger with love and smile
Love can only unite. Love gives life, hate takes life

What loved filled heart can see, one's naked eyes can't see
Like loved filled silence speak ,everyone can't hear unless in love

Blessed and lucky are those inspired by love and guided by wisdom
You being the most important person to yourself, love first yourself

Give gift of love to self. Are you aware, how lonely is your loneliness?!
Without love life will be like sunless garden. Love is like sunshine

Rivers merge into ocean, spring season brings bliss
So we say love is truth, love is sharing and love is God.

By Mamutty chola

IN SEPARATION LOVES FLOURISHES

What a pang of separation, your memory kept
Coming whole night, no end to my misfortune, I can
feel your presence within me but I can't touch you , my love.

My friend look beyond your beloved love, live life for
the deprived souls whose children grow up without
experiencing what is childhood is all about.

I have not lost hope, shall never, set back is part of life
Who has ever lived life without setback in life; be a king or pauper,
Prophets or philosophers.

This life is a gift of God. We are passengers on transit ship called time
While alive. Let us make the mother earth   cradle of peace
for humanity so that we are remembered even after we are gone.

My silence is terrified after hearing the hidden cry of the deprived
for help and succour from the century old saga of oppression born
out Ignorance and   poverty; the biggest enemies of humanity.

What to say of this desolate life without my love, even in spring
No flower blossomed, no celebration of joy still I am in autumn

While parting she asked for token of love I said, you are already
taking my smile and leaving me with hurt of separation
what more you need my love !

By mamutty chola

Paradox Of Human Relationship

*Self-interest being the core of human relationship,
we experience relationship withering away in life
when self-interests are not met.
Whom we consider our loved ones and destiny
often seen flying way like floating clouds with
changing direction of the wind.*

*So never make decisions when either
you are very happy or very sad
If you do, you will live to regret
rest of your life. Dont you read
heart breaking and shocking tales of
betrayal by loved ones in national news papers
The parents world over like gardeners
nurture their loved ones but when they
grow up fly away like migratory birds leaving
in lurch their parents who had sacrificed
everything for their betterment.
So beware; everything is transient except
self interest. Better save for rainy days to lead
a life of dignity in the twilight of your sojourn on earth.
By Mamutty chol*

FEELINGS AND EMOTIONS

Years ago I had written a letter but could not post
Today when opened after years, found writings still wet!!

After destiny parted us, I realised
How different you were from others

You would be disappointed, if you keep
Relations with weak persons in life

I meet with smile whomsoever I meet
Why to talk of autumn when you are in spring
That dreams of togetherness with love, remained a dream
Now I live in today which is a reality, gone time never comes back

I trust the language of eyes, though silent
Facial expression could be fake and acted!

The world laughs at those who fall, that is the way
Why should anyone save you, you are not a kid!!

The caravan of time never waits for any one
Whether be a king or a pauper, however powerful or weak

I have suffered so much trusting all in vain
My feelings have turned into stone, nothing affects me now
By Mamutty chola

Life Is Celebrations

Life is caravan of blessings
Life is an opportunity avail of it

Life is beautiful live it and enjoy it
Life is beautiful dream realise it

Life is challenge face it with vigour
Life is duty perform it with honesty

Life is play, play it to win throughout
Life is promise redeem it in good faith

Life is series of events face with smile
Life is a song sing it with loved ones

Life is ongoing struggles accept it
Life is tragedy as well, face it with courage

Life is confluence of setbacks, face it
Life is caravans of desires, lucks, fates

Life is invaluable gift of nature, don't waste it
Life is life protect it with all might, my friend

Life is blessing from Almighty, protect it as treasure.
Life meant it be lived with love and care for a better world.
By Mmautty chola

THE WIDENING DIVIDE IN SOCIETY

Our life journey is full of upheavals
In childhood for fantasy, in youth for dreams

In middle age for necessities and in old age for realities
Life is sum total of dreams, desires and of necessities

However, the tough time might be in life
It does pass, only tough people do survive

Life always demands sacrifice, there is no free lunch
Flowers bloom only after seeds are sown or buried

If you wish to gain success, efforts have to be put
your work should speak and not you; my friend

Do you know in the modern cities?
There are three cities within a city

Of rich, of middle class and of the poor
Each has different aspirations. and way of life

Widening gap in our society are reflections of our values
Does the slogan of inclusive development the answer????
By Mamutty chola

My Long Cherished Hope

Living with long cherished hope since years
When I could restore lost smiles of my loved ones

Every prayer, every efforts and every hopes
Have remained unanswered and unfulfilled

Like unfathomable abysm too long
How long, how long this abysm still on

Had never imaged moment's mistakes
Would result in life long agony and despair

Will ever remember lessons learned in life
Will share with loved ones, never trust even shadow

The world is full of selfish and cut throats
They live with the sole objectives of cheating others

However tough life might be, will never give up
Determined to regain lost status and fame

In the dawning twilight of my life like setting sun
I only worry for my loved ones all the times

Fail I shall not, shall not get peace even after gone
My soul will live in agony if I fail while am alive,

My prayers to God help me succeed in my efforts
Since reached end of tolerance lest I may lose faith in you!!

By Mmautty chola

MESSAGE OF LIFE

What is hope but a waking dream
Must for success in life being human

Those who say they are friends to all
In reality, they are friends to none but self

Remember always, failure is an incident
Not a defeat till you give up your fight

Those who fall and rise again and again
Can only overcome adversities in life

Mere aspirations will not make you a success
Must be gifted with qualities such as

Capabilities, integrity and self confidence
Be it an individual or a nation   for success

Firm determination, and focused vision essential
These qualities are gift of your environment and heritage

Being human, none is perfect, even Moon has defects
Still it is source of moonlight as ordained by nature

Though borrowed from sun, still generous in nature in sharing
Diamond even if defective, still is more valuable than stones

Those who have positive thoughts are always liberated in values
No wonder, such people live in harmony with self and society at large,

We are what our thoughts are; thinking makes all the difference
For that reasons, we have amidst us Gandhi and Hitler!!
By Mamutty chola

ACTS OF KINDNESS

Acts of kindness are like eternal lamp
World being self-centred , keep your expectations in limits

Value degraded, everything is on sale
Be it loyalty, trust, and love in life

Not me alone, the whole world was her fan
Her sublime qualities outshine like sun

But for the trust deficit in her,
she would have ruled millions

Why to hide, be visible to all
Every story has an end in life

Why should I blame your attitude?
There must be shortcomings in me

While alive, often ignored by loved ones
After death their photographs adored for show

If you have determination to conquer new frontiers
Invent capabilities to achieve your goal in life

Kindness effects are like river flow
Bring happiness like lush green meadows,

CONSICIENCE DIES IN SILENCE

Every murderer first murders his own conscience
Such murder happens in silence unknown to others

Why should I blame the world for my ruins?
our problems   are the results of our thoughts and actions

Your taunts every now and then; world is better than me?
Ho dear, have you found someone better than me

The world is madly in love with moonlight
Full moon is of no use to blind men in life

I love you my love from the depth of my soul
I will wait for you rest of my life **;unconditioned**

Being innocent of the ways the world, I suffered
Now I do not trust even my own shadow, my friend

Let the world know my love is mine only. no one should aspire for her
She has been, is and shall remain my first love in life always,

I am happy the whole world accept, my love is mine only
As they see in my eyes, image of her, of my love.

By Mamutty chola

March Of Humanity

Those who have left mark on time canvas
Are remembered down the ages till eternity

Lead a life   like a candle always
Which spreads light all around

Earn a status of eminence in life
Be a role model for others in life

When God is one; be it temple, mosque, church
Ho God! then why this madness of hatred among believers

It needs courage to live with smiles given
The madness of intolerance in our society

When you   raise an accusing finger at others
Remember three fingers are pointing at you

Our heart is as tender as flower filled with love
Protect it from the forces of evil designs for the sake of love

Never invite troubles by your ill-advised actions
Lest you may live to regret over your follies to no end.
By Mamutty chola

PEACE IS OMNIPOTENT

Secret of peace is hidden in live and let live principles
Failing which bloodshed, genocide and war is the option

Tolerance is key to peace; be it home, nation or world
Every human being has a right to lead a peaceful life

Saga of human civilization is witness to the fact that
There has never been a bad peace or a good war!!

Have you ever tried to fathom tolerance?
what do we mean by tolerance?

It is in our heritage to live and let live
Hallmark of our aged old culture

If there is any hurdle in our life
That is fear, a dark room where only

Negatives are developed, a debt you do not owe
To overcome fear it is essential to think positive in life

What is faith, did you ever try to fathom the meaning
Faith I believe, difficult to destroy , It is invincible

We all live under the same sky,
All have different believe systems

What is tear? Have you ever thought of it?
It is silent expression of oppressed and deprived,
By Mamutty chola

CHANGING RELATIONSHIPS

Often I wonder what is that force
Which binds two strangers in a bound of love

Love is not the only reason. for being together
Concerns, care, trust, space ,meeting of minds are

Without spirit of sacrifice no relationship will prosper
Give and take is the bounding factors which cement the relationships.
It is like gardening,24by7 attention is must

The increasing breaks down of relationship and resultant
Gulf of misunderstanding have its root in egocentric approach in life

More than love, loyalty and trust are more crucial
No relationship can last without trust and loyalty,

Every human being be it rich or poor, men or women
All want a space for self, else relationship will be of compromise

These are signs of changing time; adjustment is key, change being permanent.
Today's relationships is rooted in self-respect more than in love.

Those lives filled with concerns, mutual respects and love
Will survive any changing ups and downs and will be like a cradle of happiness in life

If you don't have care and concerns for your loved ones
Then forget about leading a happy life with your loved ones.

BY Mamutty chola

TENDER HEART

Tried many a times to build my own dream home,
Ill –luck would have it, each time I failed

The adversarial world has made me stone hearted
Any amount of offence does not affect me despite severity of the attack

, Have been unlucky, failed to meet lost love despite long wait
I would wait for her till eternity like mighty sea waves

Love does happen one cannot choose to fall in love
Love is that flame its spark once lighted, never ceases to burn

Deep down in my heart, longing does exist for my love
Her memories keep flashing in my mind's screen when I am alone

As token of love while departing she took my smiles along
It is ages since I have smiled last, yet I have to live as promised to her

we, human being are bundle of desired and unfulfilled dreams
Whether we live in palace or huts desires are unlimited

This is a part of luggage we carry from womb to tomb
For that reasons there are endless struggles since birth to death

What a hypocrisy being man of stone hearted talk of charity
And compassion sound hallows to the core; Oh man be rational
By Mamutty chola

CAUSES OF DESTRUCTION

The things responsible for destruction in the world are money, woman, land and intolerance since dawn of human life

Being human, it is impossible to escape from the spell of greed
Only those who do not cheat, who do not get an opportunity to cheat

Human history is witness to the crime committed down the ages;
be war, genocide , murder and mass destruction were the four
things mentioned above without exception; examples Alexander
or Hitler

As long as the world is divided on the ground of race, colour or religion.
The peace will remain homeless throughout the world till eternity

How I wished we men could learn how to live in peace from air and birds.
They consider the whole world their home ignoring man made boundaries

What an irony we humans are on the path self-destruction
Unmindful of the adverse consequences and ramifications

What use these wealth, status, reputation and power
If we, human beings fail to serve fellow human beings in distress

All those who work for betterment of humanity even after
They are gone, will shine ever like bright stars in the sky

By Mamutty chola

THINK HIGH ALWAYS

Always cherish high goal in life
You have faculties to excel in life

Nature has bestowed unlimited qualities in us
Nothing is impossible; if one tries to excel

If you have fire in your belly to achieve
Everything is achievable in life

When you have the urge to fly high, fly like falcon
Don't be content with crawling in life like insects

Focused action aimed at your target in life
will naturally help you gain success in life

The true lovers always see sparks of God
In their beloved since true love is God

Success is outcome of your focused actions
Nothing ventures nothing gains is a truth

Real critics are always your well wishers
So always accept well-meant criticism as suggestion

Life is not a bed of roses but of thorns, my friend
It takes years to succeed life.

Always remember, success **is earned**
Neither falls from heaven nor gets in charity

Journey of truth is hurdles ridden but
Always less crowded but full of hurdles

Tolerance is a supreme quality in life
It transforms man into angel in life

Your success is always hidden in your efforts
So keep the journey on, you **may meet success at next turn**

Life is full of ups and downs like changing seasons
Change is only permanent in life rest are all transient

By Mamutty chola

Who Am I?

I am aware of my capabilities
I am also aware of my weaknesses

I am aware of limitations of my strengths
Because I know of my shortcomings

I am fearless and fully aware each aspect of my life
I can recognise and differentiate reality and fraud

Life's experience has taught me what does life mean
I have learned from my mistakes the lessons of life

I am grateful for nature's gift and her benevolence
I have ignored and forgiven those who have harmed me

I can live with smile and without fear in my life
I understand what it means to be deprived and sadden

Life journey has been full of hurdles still I travelled alone
My life experience taught me, it is not easy to become a good human being

I wish to share two lessons of life learned with all; first
Your focus in life has to be on what is wrong and not who is wrong
2nd, if you trust people you will either get a good friend else a good lesson!!

I have learned to tolerate all in my life since long
Because there are people in my life more tolerant with me !!

By Mamutty chola

MY LITTLE DOLL-ZEENAT

She was a little doll when she came into my life
Her smile gives me inspiration to live on in life

My failures; because of my follies took her smile away
Her heart is abode of love, passion, care and concerns for all

She is exemplary in her concerns; a symbol of sacrifice
I live for her smile and pray to creator make her life abode of bliss

No words to thank creator for HIS benevolence and kindness
I am blessed with a daughter whose heart is filled with love for one and all

She means everything to me , my life, my happiness and my anchor
But for her, this life of mine would have been like lonely journey in vast empty desert

Indeed, lucky are those parents who are blessed with such adoring daughters
How unfortunate are those parents who treat their daughters as burden?

Quran says blessed is that mother whose first child is a daughter
Daughter carries tender heart with fountain of love for all; unmatched

At the dawn of twilight of my life my only prayer to God
May her life be a cradle of happiness, joy and success. Ameen.

By Mamutty chola

WE ALL ARE ONE

After death if realisation dawned of one's guilt
How is it possible to confess or atone for one's guilt?

I was unaware of impending threats on the horizon
My life was in the midst of storm in a violent sea

Those who are creating division among people based on religion or caste
Are enemies of the nation we all are first Indians then Hindu or Muslim

Beware in the self-centred world, everybody's business
Becomes nobody's business; ultimate loser is the nation

In the fast changing world; if focus is on I, me and myself
Then you are destined to fail

All relations are like bubbles and like changing seasons
You will find happiness and sorrow as transient companions

Indifference of others is expected and nothing new
Indifference of loved ones is indeed unbearable

It has been ages since I had met my own self
When happened to look at mirror I saw a stranger
Surprised I was. Asked him who are you?
By Mamuttty chola

LIFE IS GIFT OF CREATOR

It is a fact we can do anything in life
But we cannot get Whatever we desire

Those who appreciate other's success.
They find their success in others

Our conscience is chamber of justice
For that reason, conscience keeps us on right path

What is the difference between a human and a criminal
Human has conscience and criminal kills his conscience
First before committing the crime

In life events will keep on happening, action is life
we have to keep our march on; inaction is death

Our life is a gift of the creator in this world
It is up to us what we wish to be in life.
By Mamutty chola

BE A CREATOR OF ONE'S DESTINY

One who prides over being   creator of one's destiny
Are often seen   falling from fame to disgrace

Comes destruction before construction
It has been the norm in the world ever

Remember, secret of success lies in focused action
Every problem has always the solution **hidden within**

In right action lies the key to attainment of success in life
Past experience often acts as milestone in life

Fear of defeat is like cancer in life
You must bury fear to achieve success

What is one's destination in one's life
The finishing point is the destination in life

This life journey of ours is very short and transient
This journey has been on since time immemorial

Some say we would meet on the day of judgement
Some say we would keep coming again and again

Keep maintaining relations with all in life
Everything is temporary except self interest

Anger is a curse and consequence is fatal
whosoever conquers anger conquers life.

By Mamutty chola

LIFE MEANS SHARING

Life's aim is not to search self
Life's aim is to invent self

Criteria of Happy life are not long life
But quality life with vision and mission

Moment's mistakes inflict miseries for ages
Still mistakes are committed, to err is human

Your thinking makes you what you are
We all are products of our thoughts and actions
So we find Gandhi, Abraham Lincoln and Hitler

Equality is impossible in human society
Even nature does not believe in equality

However equal opportunity is a birth right
Success depends on one's capability

Acquisition of knowledge is results of hard work
Fruits of hard work are always gratifying

Education does not mean obtaining degree
But transforms a men into good human beings

Patience is gift of self-control
Reward is always sweet and satisfying

To know thyself is great wisdom
Only human is blessed with this gift
By Mamutty chola

Realities Of Life

Life and death, happiness and sorrow ,loss and gain
Are realities of life, no one can deny being facts of life

We cannot see time but it is omnipresent all around
Time is wealth, time is power, time reputation and joy and sorrow

Evil's hold is so strong on us, what a curse ,
Only those do not cheat who do not get an opportunity!!

Who says do not be a good Hindu, Muslim, Sikh or Christian
For God sake first become a good human being; message of all religions

The talks of paradise and hell are like a distance dream
Who wants to live in the make believe world of dream

Do charity let the God decide used to be the believe
Present day man wants instant gratification for help rendered

Never be a prisoner of others thought; live your life
Decide your course of direction and be creator of your destiny.

By Mamutty chola

LIBERATED SLAVES!

I often think why few are extremely rich
And majority of people are extremely poor

All because of the way we think and act
After all we are products of our thought and actions

We find people in power impose their wills on others
Need for tolerance and live and let live in society are alien to them

The biggest hurdle is wrong thoughts and actions
Truths and change have been invincible in all ages

But in our society being subjected to rule of might is right
We experience truth is under seize of falsehood since ages

Slavery stood abolished centuries ago
We still find liberated slaves amidst us!

Take a look around you will find them every where
Be it home, work places, in society and nation at large

Reasons for degradation in values in society and country
Are attributable to power being in the hands of corrupt coterie, be it politicians or business tycoons, despite **our being a democratic country**

They use power in furtherance of their insatiable greed
There is need for revolution to cleanse the ruts

The power that be, arrogate themselves as mighty sea
Forgetting people may be like drops, but sea exist within the drops!!!!

By Mamutty chola

KEEP YOUR THOUGHT RIGHT

Never say life has not been kind to you
Look around you will realise life is a blessing

Never waste today pondering over past failures
Live your life in today; gone time would never come

Never compare self with others
Every person carries a volcano within

Remember you have to be creator of your
Happiness that depends on your thoughts and actions

Ignore taunts of the world if you wish to lead a happy life
Time is the biggest healer keep pace with changing time

You are lucky to have lived a wonderful childhood
Ask those poverty ridden souls, they have grown up without childhood

Keep your struggles on you would succeed   that is my believe
Be positive, nothing succeeds like failures provided you have learnt
From your failures , life rewards   deserving, needy gets only charity

By Mamutty chola

AS YOU SOW SO YOU REAP

What I can do you can't, what I can't you can do
But together we can do wonder, do you know that?

We all have come to this world for a purpose
Make this world a better place for fellow humans

Concerns, care and empathy sound simple
But have far reaching impact on others' lives

Even if help rendered is small, if done with love
Believe me its effect will be magical on others

Yesterday is history, today is reality, my friend
Never waste today waiting for better tomorrow

I can't do anything alone, but together yes
My good deeds' fragrance is omnipresent

All your wealth, status, fame and greatness
Are meaningless, if you can't bring smile in loved ones' life

Some come to our lives as blessing and some as curse
Accept them all as your destiny and fate, my friend

If you wish to change others in their lives
What is required is, first change yourself and your loved ones

In life those who are selfish and insecure
They need your love and concerns more!!

Love unites and reinforces positive beliefs
Hate divides and reinforces negative beliefs.
By Mamutty chola

BE A GARDENER IN LIFE

Success is assured in life if
You act as gardener in life

We are not product of circumstances
Circumstances reveal our qualities

In all action one action is the noblest of all
That action is of kindness free of cost

Like lotus blossoms in marshy land
Many men of character rose from womb of poverty

Do you know what is the most responsible act in life?
To reciprocate the help received when needed most

Take it from me, they will fail who have set out to change the world
Unless they change themselves first in life as per the changed need

Wherever or whatever you are today in life
Are the results of your thoughts and actions?

Whoever has conquered fear and mistrust in life
Have always been a success in life each time and every time
By Mamutty chola

Have Feelings For Nature

World knows the depth of all the oceans
Height of the tallest mountain, Himalaya

Velocity of the wind and the temperature of the deserts
Velocity of the under currents of oceans waves

Search has been on to know the mystery of the solar systems
Have been working how to settle men on Moon and planets

Few are in search of secrets of God existence since long
We are also worried for the fast deteriorating climate

For years have been searching remedy for cancer cure
The research is also on to know about birds and animals

It is indeed a tragedy we are not concerned how to liberate
Humanity from the curse of poverty, hunger and ignorance

We may succeed only if we have feelings for our fellow human beings
Our focus has to be on to know thyself and invent themselves

Till then mother earth will suffer under the spell of men's greed
The greed based development will turn mother earth into a fire boll
Then only we will realise we cannot eat money for survival.

By Mamutty chola

Mumbai's Localtrain

Whenever I happen to travel
In Mumbai's local train

I have observed life in action on plate forms
Among travellers are old, young and children

All eagerly await arrival of their trains
Plate form is confluence of humanity

Some wait for train arrival others for loved ones
There are some lost in thought sitting all alone

You observe transactions of various types among people
Some are busy with their clients, some are lost in themselves

There are some sitting whiling away their times
When trains arrive all bogies are fully packed

It is fun to watch people trying to enter into bogies
The struggles remind me of the great human urge to survive

Inside the bogies few are sitting, rest are standing even at the entrance
Despite extreme congestion all are busy in their own worlds

Some on mobile, some on office politics, some on
stock exchange fluctuation and some lost in their worries
The sight of blind begging, hawkers selling their items
With their innovative selling and marketing strategies

Are fun to watch. Those lucky to get seats are often seen dossing
Boys and girls are seen busy in their own world least worried

You often seen youngsters indulging in stunts unmindful of risk to
Their lives and for their parents eagerly waiting for their safe returns

One aspect of train journey which touches heart is the care and
concerns Among fellow passengers for each other for helping
saving from falling

While entering or getting down despite being rank strangers
Local train is great unifiers. Life comes to an stand still without
Local train

Local train carries millions daily to their destinations to and fro
Mumbai local train is the cheapest mode of transport in the world
Even Metro arrival has not dimmed the importance of local trains

Mumbai local train is the biggest gift to the citizens of Mumbai
We cannot imagine Mumbai without local train like slum of
Mumbai!!
By Mamutty chola

SLUMS OF MUMBAI

Whenever I happen to travel in Mumbai local train
I see strange vista of slum lives of Mumbai

Whether you travel from church gate or VT
You will come across slums both sides of the rly tracks

Slums are strength of the Mumbai. It is a reality
Great personalities were born in Mumbai slums

Some became underworld kings, some became film stars
Mumbai 's life rest on slums of Mumbai, it is a fact.

Slums of Daravi is renown world over for its wonders,
These slums are cradles of harmony, tolerance and brother hood

Mumbai life is coterminous with slums of Mumbai 24X7 basis
The vibrant lives of Mumbai owe its existence to slums of Mumbai

Sky touching magnificent buildings in Mumbai have taken birth from the wombs of slums. Mumbai life is incomplete without slums.
By Mamutty chola

Mumbai's Juhu Beach

Life at Jehu is vibrant, joyous, and full of romance
Whenever happen to visit with loved ones, it is a treat to observe

Lives in bloom, gusto, action, songs of life vibrate
A sight of happiness, prosperity and urge to live

Find every one lost in their own dreams world
Be children, young couples, and old pairs holding hands

Lost in themselves away from daily worries, struggles and tensions
Playing with sea waves touching their feet; children running towards sea

Some alone some with loved ones sitting on sea shore watching
The magnificent evening sun setting scene midst red clouds,

Children insisting on joy ride on horses, buggy and swings
What children, what young and what old all crowding around
Pani puri stalls, coconut stalls forgetting their daily worries of life

There are cases of suicides who have lost interests in life
Ignoring the message of life the waves were trying to give

Waves lives are exemplary in nature, They are on struggles
Since time immemorial to cross over to the shore, each time

They fail but hey come with force again just remind us
Life means struggle and action and inaction is death

Sun setting sights ;be it Mumbai, Marina, Kovalam Port Blair,
Or Miami are priceless, beautiful, enchanting like paradise on earth

There is strong universal bounding between beaches and humanity
We human irrespective of caste creed, religion and race fall in love with beaches
Mother earth has given us so much, we as custodian have to protect nature for posterity
By Mamutty chola

From Dust You Came To Dust You Go

How strange, you externalise failures
and internalise success for self-glory

I am witness to scenes where silence reigns
Still dialogue is on uninterrupted among people

People trust palmistry blindly for insecurity
What about those who do not have hands

Whenever in life, I have had to face tough situations
Prayers of my mother have always been my refuge

Whenever I go and sit on the sea shore in solitude
There comes a voice from within ho man; you are made of
Of dust and shall merge with dust when death beckons you

I love angry mood of my love for her innocence
For she has a right to be angry with her loved ones

Ho man; do not decide your fate by tossing the coin
It is the question of your life and not that of luck.
By Mamutty chola

TRUST ONCE BROKEN, BROKEN FOR EVER

Meeting with love is always joyous
Separation in love is painful loneliness

Separation is often the destiny of true love
I beg of nature do not separate me from my love

For nature never does betray true love
So I can be with my love for ever and ,ever

The world can never feel the pain of separated
I been on move for ages in search of my love

I have faith; faith being a passionate intuition, in search
Been in different places, different people, beyond sea

If meeting happens, love is divine else
The prisoner of loneliness for life

In true love even after separation, the souls live
In each other. Soul does not believe in physical presence

If you take away love from earth
It will turn into a tomb for humanity.
By Mamutty chola

Bitter Truth

Everyone is desirous of paradise
But no one is ready to die

Never, say such thing either to me or to anybody
Which is neither true, good, right or of no use

Always remember wise listens more and talks less
It is a sign of wisdom

If there are more police than required
It is sign of curb on dissent and freedom of speech

If there are heavy movements of soldiers
It is sign of war preparedness

If there are more lawyers than required
It is sign of prolonged litigation and delayed justice

If you wish to avoid your own shadow
Then face towards the sun

As long as greed based values dominate
The poor and deprived will continue to in the grip of poverty.

By Mamutty chola

LIFE IS TRANSIENT

This world of ours is like an inn
Our sojourn on earth is like a transit passenger

Whoever comes has to go
Death is definite without exception

I wonder at times why people are so arrogant
Even a second is not within our control, power

While alive make this life memorable
Live life for self, loved ones and others

Where you will get such beautiful world
Enchanting scenery, majestic rivers, might oceans

Ice covered mountains, crystal clear streams
Live sustaining vegetation, lush green forest,

Galaxy of stars' moonlight, romantic rains
Care free birds in the sky, dancing peacocks,

Morning cool breeze, crystal dew, life enriching
Seasons of spring, rain, summer and autumn
Miles and miles vast deserts and ever changing dunes

Live life share and spread message **of love**
Our life being transient like bubbles on lake

We all come empty hands and go empty hands
Leave a mark on time canvass for posterity

Your wealth, fame, status, reputation and power
All will leave when time comes for you to depart

Message of all religion is to spread smiles and
Serve poor; the biggest service to God

When we are gone, our good deeds
will keep us alive till eternity.

NEVER LOSE YOUR INDIVIDUALITY

Never lose your individuality for false image
Success lies in inventing self to know thyself

Aim of your life is to achieve success at every step
Create self-worth by your focused actions in life

Fame, status, position and wealth you get by default
If you are a success in life .Remember talent is genetic

Never stop dreaming, it is mother of all success
It is like bird with wings; be a falcon in life

Never regret setbacks in life they are ladder to success
If learned from your failures. Success has no finishing point

you and your image are products of your thoughts and actions
Believe me, magic of success is the outcomes of your focused actions.

By Mamutty chola

War For Peace

Faith is that believe my friend
Everyone does not have faith in

War is crime against humanity
But every aggressor says he is for peace

Every one of us is product of one's environment
There are very few who are ahead of time

Always remember, future warning is hidden in today
You need to be future focused to sense the emerging trends

When every action is coloured with religious biased
Such people are beyond redemption, unless thought process changed

Our world is full of such people who are a problems in society
They make others' lives miserable who wish to lead a dignified life

Since the dawn of human civilization we, human beings are divided in the names of religion, caste ,creed, colour, the very genesis of intolerance

To work for peace is sign of humanism
A better and sane message for posterity

By Mamutty chola

Two Faced World

World of ours is of big dilemma
Those who say they love rain,
then why carry umbrella?

Some say they love wind
Then why keep windows shut?

Some say they love sunbath
Then why   search shade while waking in sun?

Therefore, I do not trust people on face value
When they say they are my friends!!

By Mamutty chola

EMERGING DREAMS

Dreams emerge daily and disappear again
Behind the shadow of oblivion for good

Why so long for good days to come; despite efforts
Every time hears knock at my door but never enters

This endless wait taking its tolls
This hide and seek is on since long

Ho life! tell me how long this wait
Is it destiny's or my fault? waited long

Admitted, I did make mistakes
That were emotional not intentional

Don't punish me for life for mistakes of moments
To err is human who had not made mistakes in life?

Youth fantasies are like floating clouds
Without focus, swayed by moment's spurs

Whom I loved from the depth of my heart
Was fairy beyond my reach like star in the sky

Says wisdom don't waste life in wait for impossible
Lest I will be left alone in the vast desert of gloom

Realisation since dawned, will not punish my life

Decided to live in today till end of my sojourn on earth

Loving all to spread message of love, love is God
Flower blossoms with sunshine of love so does man!!!
By Mamutty chola

NEVER BE SLAVE OF YOUR EGO

It is praiseworthy to keep your ego under check
Else it is a recipe for your self-destruction in life

Man of character being moral and ethical
Always uses his authority as responsibility

Any education systems devoid of ethical and moral values
Are a big fraud on the society ab initio

Ignorance is the root cause of all evils
This is the message of civilization down the ages

Men are born fee but not equal; must be understood
Even nature does not believe in equality!!

Experience tells us honesty is not the best policy
Rich peoples around the world are living examples!!

Nature's bounty is for all humanity on the earth
might is right biggest hurdles for humanity

Knowledge and wisdom are two different things
For that reasons, knowledge speaks and wisdom listens.
By Mamutty chola

THIS WONDERFUL WORLD OF OURS

Empty and egoist talks have no use for society
Unless it is beneficial to the society

Nothing is impossible for that person
Whose aim in life is perfection and perfection only

Those who live for themselves unmindful of fellow humans
There is no difference between them and lions or cheetahs

It is wrong to presume that only victors see the end of the war
In fact, only martyrs see the consequences of war

Children getting frighten by night is understandable
Grown up getting frighten by day light is a matter of concerns

Purpose of education is to spread message of humanity
That education which spreads hatred is a crime against humanity

Laws are for the safety and protection of people
Still people oppose laws which restricts regressive customs

If educated class shun politics being a dirty profession
Consequence will be; criminal will have free say in society
And in democracy you will get the government you deserve!

By Mamutty chola

Leaders; Traders In Dreams

We have leaders who promise moon
But they are like traders of dreams

There was a leader who promised
Good days for all, jobs for all

Corruption free life for all
Joy and happiness for all

When came to power
Only indulged in rhetorics

Acted as narcissistic leader
Utilised all resources for self-glory

Visited all the **countries at govt expense**
To promote self-more **less the country**

End results, jobless growth, fall in GDP
Intolerance of unprecedented scale
Worst possible relations with neighbours

Dissent treated as anti-national
Restriction of media and free speech

When nation ask where are his promises,
He indulged in rhetoric and blame games

Blames past rulers for his current failures
Maintains stoic silence on corruption

He is an expert in diversional **tactics**
He believes in his way or no way

Now nation is worried what to do with him
He has already booked a place for self in the
Hall of forgotten being a narcissist.

By Mamutty chola

Never Trade In People 'S Faith

Beware of fraudulent religious gurus; be of any faith
Those who do trade with people's faith in the name of God

When God is within you why to go on religious pilgrimage
Said Kabir, what biggest hypocrisy, despite fish living in
water how it could be thirsty!!

Listen to voice of your conscience, which is God's voice
Believe me genesis of all goodness and evils are based
on our thoughts and actions

Ho! Moon don't appear in blind men's land
They can't appreciate your charm and elegance
Though you live every one's hearts despite miles away

See the audacity of present day politicians
They are out there to sell specs to the blinds

Never make fun of less fortunate among you
Who knows they will be where you are today!!

I know one thing for sure
No one yet invented that, paper, pen and ink

Which could summarize attributes of Creator-God
Even an eternity will not suffice; however hard we may try!!!
By Mamutty chola

Your Work Should Speak

As a drop is the genesis of birth of ocean
So our good work brings happiness

When your work speaks
Your words go on long walk.

Hope is a waking dream
Hope is basis of all actions

Your faith is your saviour, it is true
But faith is not alone, but your action too

Suspicion has been incurable in all ages
It is a curse worse than poison
and reason for self-destruction

If vision is focused on goal beyond horizon
Succession will always be within the reach

By Mamutty chola

THERE ARE WORLD BEYOND STARS

Know thyself nothing is impossible
If you have self confidence
Never depends on others
Be   the creator of self-destiny

Never fear, fear is dark room
Where only negatives are developed
Ventures out in the open life is a battle field
Beginning may be small, Rome was not built in a day

But with focus on right direction
Thousand's miles journey starts with first two steps
Keep the efforts on, success will be yours
Never give up success is guaranteed

Determination and resolve be like Himalaya
Patience and perseverance key to success
Ignore the motivated criticisms of all
Trust in self, faith in self and believe in self ;essential

Failure is the first step towards success
Provided you learn from your mistakes
Invent relevant capabilities in life
If you aspire for fairy, create paradise first.

By Mamutty chola.

WONDER OF YOUTH

We all pass through three phases of life

Childhood, youth and old age

Youthful period is period of bliss all around
Full of life, dreams . actions and adventures

Behind all major inventions and achievements
Youth power have had a role dawn human civilization

Be it Alexander ,Steve jobs or set Columbus or Bill Gates
, All lovers of the world be it Romeo Juliet, Hira Ranja,

Youth is that stage of life where focus is on excellence
Want to reach to Moon and planets beyond stars

Nature's bounty and beauty would have remained unsung
But for youth power and its insatiable desire to conquer

Right heritage and values can shape the youth power
For a better tomorrow and better world for humanity

Youths with right character can transform the world into
An abode of peace, harmony, and love on mother earth
By Mamutty chola

Do Not Fool Innocents

Those who are self-centred and egoists
Better keep a distance from them in life

Modern men have crossed all limits of civility
What to talk of human, even animals are shocked?

In this era of intolerance, happened to pass by bar
Seeing the bar empty, I asked whether all have become saints

Replied the barman, when people have become
Traders of blood who is interested in wine

When frauds and cheating have become
Orders of the day, what use of honest people

The time gone by was an era of concerns and care
Now we live in era of loot, grab and greed

All are busy in I, me and myself pursuits,
Murder, rape and scams are fun games for social media

Children in slums grow up without childhood
No one is there to listen to their cry of helplessness

Happened to pass by a lane saw an old man crying
When asked said, he has become victim of bank fraud

Why these leaders indulge in false promises of Ache din!!!
Rulers are mostly traders of dreams to seize power.
By Amity choli

Who Has Time For You?

Those who love each other in life
Can only claims ownership of each other

Your tears are your companion in life
Express itself both in joy and sorrow

Those who keep pace at every step in life
Can only deserve to be happy in life

Who has time to worry about your problems
When the whole world is in the grip of gloom

Life means fun, sharing and actions
Key to happiness in all situations

I still remember that tree which would give us
Shelter from the scorching heat; when together

When found missing enquired from the wind, told that
Tree has become part of gone by time like our lost love

By Mamutty chola

KNOWLEDGE SPEAKS, WISDOM LISTENS

All your good qualities may not suffice to win over confidence
One flaw in nurturing ill-will in life
Meet with smile whomsoever you meet life being too short

What a hypocrisy, all want true friends in life
But the question is are we true to ourselves?

I have never desired for any one after I lost my love
Reason; none was of her match in grace and care

When someone asked me what is love,
I just smiled and thought of my lost love

All true men of wisdom have come to the conclusion
That they know nothing about nature 's mystery

A real sign of wisdom for that reason only
Knowledge speaks and wisdom listen!!!
By mamutty chola

Mirror And Shade Best Friends

Make friendship with people
Who have qualities of mirror and shade
Because mirror never tells lie
And shade will never leave you

When people's interest is served
They change colour very often
Hold of evils so strong on us
Only those who do not cheat
Who don't get chance to cheat

Take lesson from sun, it rises and sets
So in life ups and down integral to our lives
Those who are victims of egoist syndromes
Neither prayers nor medicines could save them.
By Mamutty chola

CONSCIENCE IS CHAMBER OF JUSTICE

My conscience being the chamber of justice
Let my conscience decides leave me alone

I never say that I am superior to you in any respects
But no way inferior either for that reason I am here

Wherever I am I will spread light like a candle
Also allow others to light their candles from my candle

For years I did't remember you my love
But that does't mean I did't remember you

Since evening I am waiting with tears filled eyes
Reason; my soul is restless for your company

I was watching from window leaves falling from the trees
This being Autumn, the trees will soon get new leaves

The seasonal changes signal; Change is only permanent
Seasons come and go but not the time gone by neither youth.

Time has, however one good quality, it never lasts; be good or bad
So we say tough time never lasts but tough people do, how true in life.
By Mamutty chola

Voice Of Reason

Neither birth nor death is in our control
We neither come nor go with our volition

If you are desirous of leading a happy and balanced life,
focus in life has to be on what is wrong instead of who is wrong.

Whether you agree or not, no creature on earth can live alone
.For that reason God has created all livings being in pairs. .

It is wrong to say that our problems are due to external reasons
we are what we are mainly based on our thoughts and actions.

The secret of success or failure depends on two factors.
Neither give excuses nor accept excuses. Please do retrospect

Language of tolerance is silence, essential in life to excel.
Tear is the best friend always both in happiness and tragedy.

Beauty without grace is no beauty and of no use.
Likewise action is life, inaction is death.

By Mmautty chola

NO ONE IS PERFECT IN THE WORLD

When no one is perfect in this world, then
why this demand for perfection from others?
The angel of peace always resides in tolerance,
Do you know? Knowledge speaks. Wisdom listens.

when you cannot keep your own secrets to self,
it is foolish to expect others to be your confidant.
Never show arrogance of your position to the less
unfortunate, who knows tomorrow they will be
where you are today.

Automation and digitization have ushered in an
era of jobless growth with impending threats to
our social fabrics in society across the globe.
Change is permanent. Resistant to change is fatal

Education systems should be like Olive tree;
ever, evergreen and relevant to the needs of the society,
Have you ever given any gift to yourself. If not
, give your today and tomorrow as gifts to yourself
and see the magic in your life. .

ByMmautty chola

Never Been Good War Or Bad Peace

Never feel jealous of other success.
Jealousy is like an ulcer which is harmful

Success has no boundaries or limits.
It is a journey of excellence.

In this world everything is subject to
change except change!!

There has never been or will ever be
good war or bad peace in human history.

Poverty has been one of the biggest enemies
of humanity. Rulers of all ages and political affiliations
have been exploiting the poor; to remain in power.

A true friend is like salt when not there, we feel it.
You must give up arrogance but not your self-dignity,

Without dignity there is no life worth living.
No one can teach lesson of loyalty better than
Postal stamp, It never leaves till the letter is delivered,

We all are destined to die, except our ideas and truth.
Nothing succeeds like failure.
By Mmautty chola

BREAKING NEWS OF 21 ST CENTURY

The biggest breaking news of 21 centuries is that
evils have taken over goodness, injustice over

justice and terror over peace. Adherence to high
values in life will determine your character in life.

Darkness gives birth to light. Like dawn emerges
from the womb of darkness.

I am a witness to that enchanting natural events;
rivers merging into sea like small babies
embracing their mothers for comfort and safety.

Do you know why all instructions in life start with NO?
Because it was the first commandment from
God to Adam and Eve while in paradise.

Have you ever thought? each of us has multiple personalities
within us —of father/mother,
husband/wife, son/daughter, brother/sister.

While dealing with persons these aspects
must be remembered for better understanding
and lasting relationship.

Man is the only creature of all of the creations
on earth who carries poison in his words.
By Mmautty chola

No Time For Self

Maintain relations with people on earth
There is nothing above in the sky my friend

The most significant events of the century
Men have forgotten each other since long

Life is a thrill of the moment
It is up to you how to spend it

It was the promise for the moment
Why should I keep it for the life
When I sat for counting the tragic events
Your thought kept coming more than the others

Modern man has everything in life
Alas! he does not have time for self in life

He is not aware how lonely is his self in life
He is lost in daily struggles of survival in life.
By Mamutty chola

WONDER OF HUMAN MIND

Our mind is free from all restrictions
All barriers are creation of our imagination

Fear, anger, stress and sadness are not personal
But are conditions of mind which are transient

Do you know one thing every human mind
Takes pleasure in doing good to others

Nothing is more noble and venerable than fidelity
Sacred endowment of human mind

It is universally known fact without exception
That human mind is influenced by propaganda.

Poetry is that domain where people
Can express their original mind without fear

Do you know idleness to human mind is?
Like rust to iron so beware

Always remember, problems exist
In human mind; be it fear or anger.

By Mamutty chola

To Sink You Need To Be Alive

The happiness I have been searching since long,
It is nowhere but within me; what a late realization!

In the bygone era, many prophets came but God was one
Modern day power brokers arrogate themselves to God

Trust me, fear is that debt which you don't own to any body
Then why people treat themselves as prisoners of fear

Before you accuse some one of betrayal ask first
Are you true to yourself before accusing others?

Don't care for the criticism of those even if they are in thousands
If they have no expertise on the subject under discussion

To sink in water, you need to be alive, you must have seen
Dead body floating. After death we are not there then why
To be afraid of death?

Our laws are like writing on the sand, customs are like
Writing on the rock. One can escape from laws but not from customs
Manuwad is the living example.

By Mamutty chola

WAR MEANS DESTRUCTION, NOT PEACE

If you tell truth each time and always
You need not remember any thing

It is true that greed is   a curse
The greedy is the most poor person in the world

Among many gifts of nature there is one which is matchless
That is called smile which can bring spring in any season

Quran says to its faithful ask God what you want
Then why this customs of going to darga or mazaar

Attitude is the prime attribute of all the human qualities
Capability, perseverance, integrity are of no use   without right attitude

If you have adversaries or even enemies; it is a matter of pride
You must have stood by for honesty and integrity in life

It is wrong to presume that soldiers love war
They know the consequences of war are destruction ,and not peace

By Mmautty chola

HAPPINESS REASON FOR BEAUTY

Whenever memories dominate your dreams,
Beware, it is the sign of giving up hope in life

If you wish to understand, then understand
Ram neither lives in Ayodhya nor Allah in Kaaba
God is within you in your feelings and soul

Never make promise when you are very happy
Nor when you are very, very sad or angry in life

Never be taken in by the outward glamour
There is no substitute to character in life

Never fear, fear is a darkroom where
Only and only negatives are developed

Beauty can be the reason for happiness
But happiness is always the reason for beauty

If you wish to know how rich you are in life
Think of those things which you own but money can't buy.
BY Mamutty chola

IGNORANCE IS BLISS

If you are happy with all in life
Definitely you have ignored the mistakes of others

If all are happy with you in life
Reasons, you have tolerated weaknesses of all

Of course my mother was illiterate but
She could read the minds of others

How come this changed attitude of yours of late
Is this changed attitude a sign of revenge?

All murderers first murder their conscience
before murdering others. Such murder is so silent
no one can ever hear it happens

My soul tells me daily, my body is like a prison
Once she departs from my body would request God
Not to give such Imprisonment again in next life

Every broken thing in the world can be repaired
Except the trust once broken can never be healed

Do you know the difference between a mirror and wine?
Mirror reflects external and wine internal qualities.

By Mamutty Chola

Ho God You Are Merciful

What is memory, have you ever thought of it?
Memories are like family photo album

It has been, since long I am sad at heart
When asked for reason, came the reply
no peace at heart, reason not known

Have you ever seen rusted lock discarded?
Don't live life of rusted lock; life means action

Memories are always our permanent co-travellers
Don't live a life of prisoner in the prison of memories

All worship rising sun, but sun does set in also
No night is permanent, it has to make way for day break

Do you know sea drop is not a mere sea drop?
The whole existence of sea is within the sea drop

Ho God that hand which stretches before you
never create conditions when I have to stretch
my hands before others; you are all merciful.

By Mamutty chola

SUCCESS IS A JOURNEY

Relation in love is like a floating clouds
After short sojourn together flew away like floating clouds

Life's journey is like flow of the rivers
Never stops like a burning candle till dawn

Unaware the waves are, their death is hidden in their success!
They remain protected so long as in the lap of the sea

If you live in the memory of your love like a prisoner
Beware you will be left alone in the journey of life

It is wrong to presume success is final destination
In this fast changing world, all successes are like transit camps

Every evening walk I would see
A tired sun setting in to rise again

These promises of life long company till death
Are like floating clouds, accept the one who is your destiny.

Curse Of Hate

We hate those qualities in a person
Which are in abundance in us as well

I am free from all prejudices
My criterion of hate is truth and truth only

Strange is the human nature
In the absence of hate target, we hate ourselves

Why waste this transient life in hate?
Let us forget hate and live for love

Hate is not gate way to happiness and bliss
It is the short cut pathway to hell

The genesis of hate is frauds and cheating
Hate takes life, never gives life

Hate is that fire never leaves any one
Not only men but dirt coming its way

Do you know one reality about hate?
It corrupts not only our thought but personality also

What types of people are they who nurture?
Hate knowing well, hate takes life, never gives life

Have ever seen two enemies living together in peace
You will find love and hate in broken hearts together.

By Mamutty chola

RELATIONSHIP IS LIKE GARDENING

Mirror does't lose its characteristics despite breaking into pieces
Rather emerges into several pieces retaining its original characteristics

I am witness to several scenes of human dilemmas
There is pin dropped silence all around still dialogue goes on in silence

What to talk of lady luck knocking at my door?
It has been ages since winds have changed its directions towards my abode

How can I say I am tired of struggles and the adversities in life
Given my commitment for my loved ones, how can I thing of giving up

Whoever is blessed with qualities of patience, and silence
He understands the intricacies of life better than others

Death is ill-known for her rightful performance of her divine duties
As ordained by divine. Life being a worst task master is
lapped up as darling in life what an irony of human life

It is not at all difficult to build relations in life
But majority of us fail in nurturing the relations

Caring of relationship is like a gardening in nature
All time attention on 24X7 is prerequisite in life .
By Mamutty chola

TRUTH IS ALWAYS LONELY

Truth is always bitter for that reason always alone
Falsehood always busy in celebration like thunders

When no one is perfect in life then why
this insistence, all should be perfect in life?

Time is that earth quake under which, not only human
But their unrealized dreams lie buried deep down

Before your breakup think once again, leaving all
She came with you to be with you rest of her life till death
Think of that moments of bliss also spent together

It has been long since destiny parted us apart
But I still see her deep down in my heart's screen

I love darkness of the night because but for darkness
How could we enjoy the beauty of moon, stars and galaxy

I am tired of talking to my loneliness all alone
Even my memories have become faded and dim

The dry leafs of Autumn give us message, change is life
Don't feel sad for them, they would come again in spring .

By Mamutty chola

Life Is A Good Teacher

It is wrong to presume all smiling faces are index of happiness
I have seen many smiling faces who cry while in solitude

Saying goes before construction, destruction comes
But heart once broken can't be healed again

What types of people are they
Who spread hatred in the name of nationalism

Life teaches all one thing for doing good things in life
we can do it without money, intention matters

All rest on your thinking
Life is nothing but our thoughts

Two things can always be reasons for self-destruction
First curse of poverty and second egoistic behaviour

Every new idea is not worth consideration
Unless it has spark of changes for the better

Those who learn from mistakes are wise
Those who fail to learn become lesson for others

By Mamutty chola

Tears Are Language Of Silence

Never break mirror for your ugly look
Ho man, mirror's **existence is truth and truth only**

Secret of my sadness; couldn't wipe out tears of innocents
Still I did care for oppressed whenever opportunity came

I am afraid and I am not answerable to people in the world
When final decision rests with Almighty on the day of judgement

This tantrum of yours you would leave me, think twice
Life's relationships are like gardening; rests on give and take

If you could restrain your emotional outbursts, even for a second
Believe me, you can avert avoidable tragedies in life journey

Tears are language of silence but
Tears of the poor; language of helplessness

Sea thinks sea drops owe their existence to her
Not knowing, the very existence of sea is within the drop

You despite being mine, you never extended your hands
I have seen strangers saving unknown souls from being drawn!!
By Mmautty chola

CRITERIA OF SUCCESS

It is necessary to decide before you undertake any assignment
What should be the criteria for attainment of the goal

Your position is to be treated as responsibility
Your position is not to be treated as an authority

Set back in life is an event and not a defeat
Failure to be treated as stepping stone for success

It is a fact leaders emerge based on their merits
They neither fall from heaven nor available on charity

Your manner of talk will determine your upbringing
Also helps to determine one's background

All problem can be resolved amicably
Provided you are focused and determined

If you wish to be recognised as man of worth
First create capabilities to deserve to be considered

It is well established fact that
ill mannerism is a recipe for self-destruction

Don't waste you're today waiting for tomorrow
Today is the reality, tomorrow never comes

Those who have firmed faith in their dreams and vision
Sure to conquer new frontiers in their struggles in life

If you aim at moon, stars and planets beyond the sky
Create capabilities and qualities like falcon to fly high.

Dogs Are Best Friends

Dogs are eternal friends of men
There is no psychiatrist like our dogs

They give unconditional love
They are the role model to be
emulated
My dog Bozo was like son to me
Our love for our Bozo was infinite
He left us for his heavenly abode
leaving us in tears

What an irony being my best friend
he was not able to talk but would convey
his feelings of love through his tail

Dog can feel our feelings and console us.
We, men are no match in loyalty, care and
love when compared with dogs

They don't know evil or jealousy or
discontent. They know only love
Thorn may hurt you, your best friend
may leave you but your dog will
remain with you till last day

Your dog would wait for you
as my Bozo would do till you come
back from work When you go with

your dog to country side and play with
him in lush green meadow it is like be in heaven.
BY MAMUTTY CHOLA

Inspiration From Lion

If circumstances compel you to become
an animal then choose to be a lion.

Live and lead a life of dignity and valour
like lion than live and die like coward

The wicked attack you from behind the back
Be bold, and face life like a lion from front

The truth is like a lion, it can defend
itself in all situations since truth is power

Never pick a fight with a lion
If you are not a lion yourself

Be a lion and face the adversities in life
Like a lion rather than wait for help in vain in life

An ignorant friend to be feared more than
A lion to avoid avoidable misfortune in life

The power of our enemy lies in our fear of him
Like our fear of lion in life.
By Mamutty chola

THEIST, ATHEIST AND AGNOSTIC

The brightest side of an atheist is
He is free from religious prejudice and bigotry

An atheist lacs belief in god and no faith in god
I admire the honesty of the atheists; they are not indecisive
Like agnostics who are like fence sitter

An atheist faith in the absence of god is as strong as
The faith of theist in the existence of god

Who says an atheist does not have believe systems?
Their believe in non-existence of god is their faith!!

Unlike all the religions in the world only
Atheism is a non-prophet organization
But have their bible--- the Origin of Species

If you come to think certain distortions
In religious scriptures; are the genesis of atheism

There are three classes of believers who can be categorised
As theists, agnostics and atheists known to human civilization

Given the genocides being committed since the dawn of
human civilization in the world in the name of religion
the absence of religion is welcome and that's a wonderful thing

In retrospect, I must say faults are not of religions
We men being homo sapiens possess gene of destruction.

By Mamutty chola

MADE FOR EACH OTHER

Oh men! you are reflection of universe
Look within to fathom meaning of life
You are the best creation of all creations!

The sculptor carves his love out of stone
Be a   sculptor thyself, liberate your love hidden in rocks

Oh soul why do say my body is a prison
When I have given you shelter for life
Why can't we live in peace together?
While together during this sojourn

Oh Moon, oh stars, oh sky we men live to admire your
Eternal beauty. come to think of, but for us, your adoring
Charms would have remained unsung and gone without praise!

Oh saint don't defame wine. she is the truth
If you are with her, you would always speak truth.!

Oh men woman is your mirror, don't break her
You would never realise your worth without her!

Don't you know Adam's life was incomplete without Eve
Even in paradise. You both are made for each other.

Mamutty chola

LIVE LIFE WITH A MISSION

Never waste your life thinking of paradise
In next life. This life is reality. Make this a paradise
For self and loved ones and fellow human being

Everything is today. Time flies faster than you could
Imagine.Time is wealth, power, fame .Time is a transit ship
We are not crews but mere passengers. Our stay is a sojourn on earth

Oh men you come alone depart alone, death is only certain
If you want to become immortal, earn place in people hearts,
spread smile. Time gives opportunity to all. Be a gardener
Respect nature, nurture and protect it for next generation

Our yesterday is history, tomorrow is dream. Today is reality
Gone time never comes back, seasons do come back. Learn from
Mistake.cultivate water like qualities for adaptability, Never be stone
and remain fixed with immune to changes, sure signs of death,

Ignite the fire of action in your heart, Keep the imagination
fly high like falcon to reach moon, stars and planets.
New world awaits those who have guts to venture out.

By Mmautty chola

FIGHT FOR EQUALITY IS AGAINST NATURE

Life without passion for humanity is no life at all. Life spent for self is like writing on sands, water, wind and on clouds. Life spent for fellow human is like writing on the rocks for posterity.

Make every day a memorable day with focused action
Don't worry about dead yesterday, unborn tomorrow
Make today the mirror of tomorrow by vision focused action
Then a better tomorrow will emerge from today's womb

What a tragedy most among us spend our today like the prisoner of our past forgetting our present and uncertain future, resulting in being left behind at the mercy of time, sow the seeds now if you want to reap fruits in the twilight of your life and even after you are gone

Nature is kind, benevolent and judicious ,for your one seed sown in returns you will be rewarded with thousands **of fruits.** Also be aware all time is good time, if your intentions are bona fide and honest

When we are born we come to the world with our fist closed Declaring to the world, here I come to conquer but after our sojourn Most of us depart with unfinished mission buried deep down our hearts Still some become king, some pauper. Some rich, some ,handsome Some ugly.

For that reason I say even nature does not believe in equality. We all are born free but not equal.!!! Fight for equality is a fraud

There is no equality even under communist regimes claiming to be for the poor and down trodden. Equal opportunity yes, and we must fight for being our birth right.

By Mmautty chola

OUR LIVES ARE TRANSIENT LIKE SPARKS

Of all the books ever written by men the book of love is invincible and everlasting,
It contains wisdom based on human civilization, If you want to live in peace follow book of love .It is for all time and for all humanity on mother earth.

Do you know moon has black spots on her chest, She been taking all hurts to her heart still spreading love .She is symbol of love ,inspiration for nations, poets and lovers.She resides in our hearts being miles away . The full moon light is blessing for mother earth, She shares her beauty and light with all, despite her light being borrowed from sun!

Youth is the best period of life, full of fun, hopes, determination to conquer new frontiers for humanity. youth, once gone never comes back unlike old age; once comes never leaves .Our lives are like bubbles , transient and passing.
We men are like passenger on transit ship called time.
No one is perfect except nature—we call God.

Do you know sea is nothing but sea drops. Earth we come from and earth we go to. The mother earth is like an inn for us. This journey of ours is a never rending till eternity... Remember, no one is indispensable. Our lives are like sparks; very transient like rainbow.
Mamutty chola

Change And Self Interest Only Permanent

Nothing is permanent except change and self interest.
Whoever could balance the two dynamics, can be a victor in life

Oh man, when you can't confine your secret to self how could you expect anybody else could be your confidant!!

Never become a prisoner of your memories.
If your memories come to dominate your dreams,
then you are heading towards road to oblivion in life,

Solitude is a well-protected abode of lonely souls
fired with dreams to excel in life for betterment of humanity.
All great religions, and all path breaking inventions since taken birth in the womb of solitude. Loneliness is like a dark room where only negatives are developed whereas solitude is an Olympian arena

Genesis of all evils is rooted in ignorance, poverty and hunger.
Hallmarks of all backward societies or nations in the world

Never impose your views on your children. let them live their dreams. They belong to new age and new era free from your prejudices and biases. Never stifle their hopes and aspirations; lest you may lose them for good.

By Mamutty chola

HOMO SAPIENS ARE DOMINANT

Message of all religions is love, peace, tolerance but
Men being homo sapiens, the urge to dominate others is inborn
In men's DNA, the very genesis of war and genocide in the world.

The world has been busy in discovering mystery of God.
I am busy in discovering self-know thyself.

The new world order of tolerance will remain a dream, unless
Our thoughts process of inclusiveness become an article of faith of humanity.

The great nations are born in the visions of poets and philosophers and prosper and decline in the care of politicians.

First deserve, then desire ,if followed as guiding principle
Journey of life will be a smooth passage in all situations; with success.

You are what your thoughts are. If you have no control over your thoughts process, you are sure to be destroyed.

If she is destined to be yours, let her go, she will come back. However, if she is not yours, even if she is with you, she will never be yours .
By Mmutty chola

NATURE'S BENEVOLENCE

No vessel can take more than its capacity
Same is our lives; be it happiness or sorrow
Excess will over flow,

Creation is an act of nature and will continue till eternity.
End of creation means end of universe,

Simplicity is not an acted behaviours but a natural
Way of life still alive ,

Take life as it comes. Even darkness gives you opportunity
to enjoy beauty of moon, stars and galaxy in the night,

Two side of the river never meet but you can reach other side
by crossing the river; not otherwise,

Try to live life like butterfly every second with joy.
However transient its sojourn might be,

Faith is that believe we men can sustain
all adversities in life with smile,

Love means sacrifice but not unconditional
it demands fidelity and loyalty on 24X7 basis
like gardening,

Real education transforms a man into
a good human being with feel for
Humanity and nature..
By Mamutty chola

NEVER CHANGE YOUR VALUES

When love is rooted in soul, lovers merge
Into each other losing their identity
and become eternal like eternit

Paradise is an illusion of bliss , Ecstasy
and flight of imagination beyond horizon
In the realm of dreams

-There is no finishing point in pursuit of
excellence. It is a never ending journey
All successes are like transit camps
changes being permanent

Beauty of death is she keeps reminding
You of good qualities of departed loved ones

My life is amazed at my determination to
fly high like falcon beyond moon, stars
and galaxy where new world awaits
humanity with new dawn

A person's popularity is not known when
he is alive but in his death. Like a true friend
who cares for you when you are down

In my madness I adored her like god
But got a shock when she said, remember
God does not belong to one but to all

Remember, never ill-treat the less privileged
Who knows one day they would be where
You are today, my friend.
By Mamutty chola

EQUALITY IS IMPOSSIBLE

People seldom do walk the talk. They do what suite them
Then live to regret whole life blaming their destiny as escape route.

All the talk of equality is a fraud because in the entire
human civilization, never equality was a guaranteed right.
Even nature does not believe in equality.
Equal opportunity yes as we all are born free but not equal!!

Laws are meant for law breakers. If one acts ethically
and morally one is not required to be afraid of any law,

Whatever might be the systems of governance;
be it democratic, autocratic, oligarchic or dictatorship;
the sole object is to control power for self-benefits by those in authority

Money is like fairy.everyone loves to have her.
Money can unite all being secular but religion can't.
By Mamutty chola

What Is Hope?

Hope is that lane which does not have a turning
Hope believes path to paradise is through hell
Hope is co-traveler but a not a friend
Hope, if trusted, is source of motivation else a dream
Hope is a waking dream
Hope is the foundation of all actions in life
Hope is there life is there
Hope creates future
Hope dies we die
Hope's traders are merchant of dreams.
By Mamutty chola

No Success Is Infinite

From the womb of failure
Emerges victory in life

The courage which is boisterous.
Can only conquer new frontier

Courageous are not intoxicated with elixir
in life but inspired by vision

Be alert on any excessive caution
Never say never, nor be diffident

Be on guard of your self-respect
Don't be a slave of others ideas

Never restrict your vision of success
Every success is a transit camp

Excellence is a continuous journey in life
Nothing is permanent but change

When adversities exceed your patience
Turn the adversities into opportunities

Remember, no success is infinite
Keep the struggle on; action is life.
By Mamutty chola

TRUE RELIGION IS HUMANISM

If you want to remain happy in life, limit your desires
and aim at those within your capabilities.

Power exercised for the betterment of society at large
are welcome, even if at the inconvenience of few.

Those who live and fight for their selfish ends
are no better than animals

All good things in the world are creation of noble souls
always dedicated to humanity and mother earth.

No pain is worth enduring unless end result
is bliss, happiness and freedom

When people are religious, it is the victory of truth and
When people are communal, then defeat of humanism.

By mamutty chola

EQUALITY Vs EQUAL OPPORTUNITY

I often wonder why there is no equality
even in nature's creation
Despite living under the same sky,
still no two persons are alike.

The aged old slogan that people **are**
born equal is a historical blunder!
Of course we all are born free but not equal.

Therefore, those who ask for equality are wrong!!!
Focus has to be for equal opportunity.

All must get equal opportunity ;yes.
That must be guaranteed to one and all

To excel in life based one's capability.
clamour for equality does arise when

citizens are denied **even equal opportunity**
guaranteed under the constitution.

Past Is A Dead Yesterday

Nothing is impossible for the right attitude
Everything impossible for the wrong attitude

Moral says honesty is the best policy, reality says
not always true, see the rise of rich people in the world

Those who live in the magic of dreams always conquer
New frontiers, rather than those who live in their past laurels
Past is a dead yesterday.

In the matter of style follow water and in the matter
of principles be like rock come what may

Differentiate between work relation and personal relation
Work relation is transient and personal relation rooted
in trust and mutual interest. Hence permanent.

Travelling alone is always inspiring and enriching rather than
travelling in company.

Power if used as responsibility is a blessing
If used as authority, then a tyranny and oppression.
By Mamutty chola

GENIUS HAS LIMITATION, STUPIDITY NONE!!

The other day my daughter
asked me, papa how do I define
initiative? I said, initiative means doing
things without being told.

Genius has limitation but Stupidity has none
Hence found in abundance every where

Being life partner, if you can't understand
Language of silence you will never understand
words either

Remember always, foundation of future edifice
of happiness is always laid today.

Sun setting and rising is an inspiring example.
Rise and fall is an integral part of human existence

There is one thing in life which is available free of cost
To one and all and is called time. Time means wealth and power,

Mob is irrational in its behaviours, if provoked
Mob becomes mother of all tyrants

There is a fixed time for supper for rich
For poor when he can afford it.
By Mamutty chola

MYSTERY THY NAME IS WOMAN

Mystery of woman is she is meant to be loved
and adored and to be understood

Women are better strategists in winning
the confidence of men and then blocking their exits

When I was young I believed that money
Unites, but know I realised it is a cause of crime

In life man takes risk in marriage
Whereas woman tries her luck

Real romance is not falling in love
with your girlfriend but falling in
love with self to explore unexplored
within you

Those books termed as immoral are
the mirrors of the society we live.

By Mamuttychola

WORDS OF WISDOM

There is one thing common between books and mines
Former with wisdom and the latter with wealth
Both are useless unless utilised

What to do with those fools
Who sit in darkness ,though can put on light

Oh my friend, don't pretend to be busy
I have ignored your indulgences since long

There were inexplicable silence and gloom
With her advent life became meaningful again

Seeing the adverse effects of intolerance
Let loose by those in power in hubris

Said I to sea waves don't become destructive
When we men are on the path of self-destruction
Which is far more destructive than your storms

Agreed, I can't stop impending storms spreading darkness
But I can definitely light few candles to keep darkness away

Even the birds don't make nests on the withering trees
Why to blame men for their selfish attitude, it is but natural
To jump out of sinking ship before it is drawn in the sea

Among the various gifts of nature one is exceptional
That is called smile it can give the comfort of spring in all seasons.

By Mamutty chola

Genius Is A Superman In A Man

Only noble souls can be poets
They live in the hearts and minds
of people till eternity; examples
are Rumi, Amir Khusro,Ghalib. Khalil Jibran
Omar Khayyam, keats, Byron and others

Many achievements are the results
of small ideas like a seed transforming
into a big trees.

For thinking person idleness
is the worst punishment
like solitary confinement,

Rhyme is the soul of poetry, is
all powerful and invincible; can
inspire king and pauper alike.

Sign of wisdom is that the more you
learn the more you feel you are ignorant.

Aim of life is not to achieve something but to
become some one of value to humanity.

Genius is not first among men but
a superman in a man.
Supreme happiness in life is that

realization that you are being loved
for your sake without any ulterior motive
despite your many shortcomings.

Habit formation has to be nurtured
and taken care so that children with
right values are developed for their
betterment and that of society.
As saying goes habit is the nursery
of deviant behaviour.
By Mamutty chola

REALITIES OF LIFE

If there is no music in life
Such life is like abyss of a vast desert

Lack of love is not the reason for bitterness
Absence of friendship is the reason for aloofness

Life is a caravan of struggles
Compromise is the name of life

Those who know why they are alive
They know well how to live life

Any relationship founded on friendship
Sure to survive all eventualities in life

Journey of truth is never a waste
Sure to reach your destination

If you can't control self
Always be at the mercy of world

Those who think out of the box,
Found often doing wonders in life

It is matter of serious concerns
Who made the mistakes?
God; by creating man or
Man; by creating God

If you wish to leave a mark on time canvass
Always act as per dictates of your conscience

If there is demand for proof for each action
Better to give up when trust deficit reigns supreme

Oh priest, stop your sermon
Which has no message of peace

The difference between loneliness and solitude
The former is living without hope and latter with full of hopes

Nothing in the world is a permanent reality
Nor there is an eternal truth in life except change.
By Mamutty chola

Life Is A Gift Of Nature

Life is an opportunity avail of it
Life is very beautiful, enjoy it

Life is a beautiful dream, fulfil it
Life is challenge, face it

Life is duty, perform it with sincerity
Life is game, play it with fun and gusto

Life is promise, redeem it with honesty
Life is full of turmoil live with smile

Life is song, sing it with your loved ones
Life is a never ending struggle, live it bravely

Life is a tragedy at times, tolerate it with grace
Life is also like tsunami, must brave it with courage

Life is bundle of luck, fate, destiny
depending on your thoughts and actions

Life is precious, and invaluable never waste it
Life is life preserve it for spreading love and peace

Life should be lived as role model for fellow humans
Life aim should be leave a better world for posterity.
By Mamutty chola

DO CHANGE YOUR OPINION, NEVER VALUE

Times caravan never stops for no one
Be it a king, or pauper ;for no one

When an idea is born
It captures world without force
It has been the saga of truth
In all ages and in all civilization

You feel delighted being loved
For your sake with carefree abundance

There is no bigger joy than to live
In people's hearts, we all live in our homes

Do you know the biggest warrior on earth?
It is not time but your patience damn it

God's creation is infinite, men's
Flight of imagination is finite

Change your views with time but not values
Change your styles but not your personality.

By Mamutty chola

MEN'S STUPIDITY IS INFINITE

No one can live alone, every one
Wants to be loved and being in love
For that reason, nature has created all
creatures in pairs, be it human, animals or insects.

Even those madly in love when separated
Find their soul mates forgetting those
Promises of life together till death.

There are still some sentimental fools
Who live in the memories of their first love
hoping for reunion like river of two banks
which are never destined to meet!!

To cover up their sense of loss they have
Invented immortality of souls and dream of
meeting their first love either in
next life or on the day of judgement.
No wonder, men's stupidity is infinite.

By Mamutty chola

Silence Is God

Silence is that lesson which whoever
has read, read very often wrongly

One who does not know how to remain silent
Will never know, either how to speak

Beware of nature's silence who knows
what is hidden in nature's silence

When silence reigns
Oppression also reigns

Silence is not only assertive
But musical as well

Silence's screams are soundless
Those who fail to understand language of silence,
Will they ever feel the pains expressed in words?

Such silence is not justified,
if it covers up truth in life

I have seen him sitting very often, on sea shore
In silence and talking to sea waves lost in his thought.
By Mamutty chola

Trust Is Two Way Traffic

To test whether you can trust someone
The best option is to trust him;
taste of pudding lies in eating

If you wish to live with smile,
First learn to trust self in life

Trust is foundation for every
Lasting relationships in life

It takes years to build your image
But does't take a split of second to lose

If you want to win over some one's trust
Rescue him from falling; be it an unsolicited act

Trust is like a two-wheeled vehicle, both have to be
Functional then only vehicle will move smoothly.
By Mamutty chola

REVENGE IS A TWO-EDGED SWORD

If we live to avenge, our world will be a battle
Ground, and destruction all around

Anger, hatred, and feelings of revenge
If nurtured, will transform you into
a stone hearted person, disliked by all
and loved by none

Revenge kills your conscience first
Before killing others; revenge is blind

Not forgiving means harming
self before harming others

The best revenge is to forgive
Your tormentor like Jesus did

Path to revenge will surely lead
You to hell; within this world

Beware of the tolerant man,
If he does explode, will explode
Like a latent volcano with mass
destruction

Never add fuel to revenge
Lest it may destroy the innocents as Well.

By Mamutty chola

HUMAN CIVILIZATION

In democracy the people elect the govt of their choice.
Therefore, they can't accuse the govt in power of being victims
If you ask me, people are not victims but accomplices!!

Why any government in power dislike truths because truth
is always bitter. It requires courage to be frank and honest
when power that be is at fault.

Self-interest being permanent till eternity, all acts of human beings
Are self-directed and rooted in personal gains since dawn of
human civilization.

Political language is designed to make lies sound truthful and
Genocide respectable aimed at radicalization of human society
To justify oppression of dissent in any authoritarian regime.

If any government which substitutes facts with fictions
and mythology, such acts not only deprive the posterity
but also the present generation of the wisdom of the past.

Minorities world over are discriminated and suppressed
Under all types of regimes since dawn of human civilization
Human being homo sapiens, minorities are destined to suffer
Till eternity!!!
By Mamutty chola

SELF INTEREST SUPREME

Whenever I sit back alone, and reflect on
Human relationships, I realise nothing is
permanent except self interest.

People come and go like floating clouds
Some leave behind traces of rains other
Shades and still other darkness all around.

In reality, nature has created all creatures in pairs
No one can live alone. All talk of eternal love, life
Together till death does us apart are empty talk.

Lovers meet, lovers depart. No one dies for each other
At the most few drops of tears like morning dew.

Those who spend their whole life in wait
Alone in memories of lost love are left alone
At the twilight of their lives like a pol star
No one to care for and being loved .

Never allow your memories to dominate your
Dreams in life,If you wish to live your life with smiles.
All talks of immortality of love and inseparable love
are in reality infatuations and obsessions of life.

Modern lovers are like dune in vast desert, keep
changing shapes as per the direction of winds!!

Magic Of Love Is Infinite

Ultimately whosoever becomes your partner in life,
Fall in love with and treat him /her as your destiny
Today is the reality past is shadow , one cannot live
With shadow like one can't live in a palace built in the air!!
By Mamutty chola

POWER OF COURAGE IS INFINITE

Courage does not mean you are not afraid of fear
Courage means your are ever ready to face the challenges

Fear is reaction, courage means action.

Courage means go ahead with your action
Irrespective of the consequences of your actions .

If you keep your boat anchored on the river bank,
How could you reach your destination, oh man ,have courage

Courage is that velour that inspires one
How to overcome the adversities in life?

Oh man of courage, never takes politeness as weakness
Only the civilized know the value of the manner

Dreams are like wings which empower ones to
Fly high above the sky like falcon in the sky;,
all depends on courage.

By Mamutty chola

ENTHUSIASM KEY TO SUCCESS

A person with values and believe is far superior
To thousand others who only have interests

Always dream big. Dreams are like wings
Which can take you very high beyond horizon
To a new world awaiting your arrival. While
dreaming big, never miss the ground realities
including your capabilities.

Enthusiasm is key to success, all others qualities are
of no use without enthusiasm; fire in the belly.

We all must have goal in life; be a king or pauper
Otherwise it will be like journey without a destination
Like a life boat in turbulent sea at the mercy of violent sea waves.

Our incredible mind; if utilised effectively can transform a person
From rags to riches, from oblivion to glory, failure to success;
with trust in self, of course , being the prime focus.

Nothing is impossible, what is required is focused endeavour
With well-defined road map keeping mind dynamic of change
Since all success are transient; change being the permanent.
By Mamutty chola

Real Freedom

No one can be a better advisor to you
than yourself in life. Do reflect on it
when you get time.

If your external environment is regressive, progressives
ideas will be nipped in the bud like toxic rains which kill
all vegetation.

No man is free if he is not the master of his destiny
Even if he lives in free democracy with guaranteed
Fundamental rights to speech.

We are like magnet. Attracts people of our nature.
For that reason we do not get along with all, being
incompatible in nature.

Whosoever can control one's thought is
A real free man.

Remember always, your tones of voice are
the barometer of your relationships with others in life

A life is an opportunity to experiment your faculties
of mind to leave a mark on the canvass of time for posterity
Human civilization is replete with such saga of achievements.
By Mamutty chola

MIRACLE OF STRUGGLE

Whosoever have achieved success
In life; be it prophets or kings
All have passed through struggles.

One who never supported you when needed
Can't expect to share glory in your success.

Never undermine others efforts and struggles
who knows they would be where you are today!!

Perform your duty well, if you are success
You work will speak, you need not speak.

No success without efforts those who
Fail to make efforts will end up in oblivion.

Before achieving success, you have to conquer self
The first step towards achieving your goal in life.

Success is the results of your struggle
No success possible without efforts in life.

Life struggle is like climbing the hill top
The journey of struggle to top is always exciting
Given the scenic beauties from the top of the hill
And when the success is within your reach.
By Mamutty chola

Compromise Is The Name Of The Marriage

There is one place your complete security on 24x7 basis is assured
But no freedom. Guess   which is that place ?Prison damn it!!

Give and take or compromise is the name of life.
In marriage, if both the partners are not forgivers,
their happiness will be very short-lived.

Kindness is a universal language like love
Which is omnipresent in our life from womb to tomb.

Music is the language of soul.
It does not believe in barrier of any kind;

Be it religion, region, caste or sect and
resides within us and unites us all.

Failure though, hurts but
very kind and considerate

Gives us opportunities again
and again to prove our worth.
By Mamutty chola

SETBACK IS AN EVENT NOT DEAEAT

There is no night without a day
Never give up, success is yours

Treat each threat as an opportunity
Every set back is not a defeat

Every setback is like ladder to success
These have been the tales of all victories

Every successful person lives with
A saga of trials, turbulation and setbacks

Greatness is never thrashed upon
It is always achieved; be a prophet or king be

Those seen with firm resolve, often
Come out with flying colour from each trial

Test of courage lies in rising up from each fall
Test of a courage lies in ultimate victory

In your problems are hidden your victory
All great victories are saga of human trials

Setbacks are never defeats in life
Giving up fight is indeed defeat.
By Mamutty chola

Power Of Ideas

No army on earth can reverse the tides
Of new idea whose time has come.

People with ideas are the real power
Who can change the world by sheer use of their ideas.

All great inventions in human history have had its
Origin in the great ideas of the inventors.

Weapons of mass destruction is no match to the
Power of new ideas which can make our world a
Better place for humanity than what we have inherited,

A good idea is like a seed, if sowed, watered and tendered
Can grow into a huge tree with great height and width.

If necessity is the mother of invention, great idea is
Grandfather of all inventions in human civilization.

Great things are achieved not by physical power
But by sheer knowledge and judgements of the inventors.

Every things in our possession today; be wealth, power,
Items of comforts, mode of transport, entertainments
Social media, internet are products of new ideas.

Every idea gives birth to new idea by way of
Innovation, creativity or invention.

By Mamutty chola

POWER OF SACRIFICE

Realization of your dreams is possible
If there is an unrelenting spirit of sacrifice within you.

Love means unconditional surrender
Since love always demands sacrifice.

Every new idea is termed as blasphemy, if it is
Contrary to religious faith.Galileo had to suffer
life time house arrest for telling the truth that
it is not the sun which rotes around the earth
but earth rotates around the sun.

Intensity of your love determines
the extend and depth of your sacrifice.

We all live for self, if we live and die for others
That is real sacrifice and we will always live in
In others hearts even after we are dead and gone,

The recent examples of Ankit saxena of Delhi and
Imam Imdadul Rashidi of Asansol Mosque , west Bengal
even after losing their young sons in communal
hatred; appealing for peace are sacrifice of unparalleled scales.
By Mamutty chola

One Who Is Afraid Will Tell Lie

Conquer your anger
You can conquer the world

Life is a battle
Victory is possible in battle field
Not in the cradle of comfort

Never give up in crisis
When you look back later you would realise

Formal education can guarantee a career
Worldly experience can give you wisdom
Which can help you gain position in society

One who is afraid will only tell lie
One who is not afraid will never tell lie

Be respectful to that person who
Listens, who thinks and who observes.
By Mamutty chola

Change Is Life

Spent my live with loved ones like stranger
Despite residing on the river banks, I remained thirsty

Years ago a spark of happiness did shine in my life
Since then it has been darkness all around

All these acts of love, being part of loved ones
All sound hallow, here who cares without motives

Been deprived of love, affection, cared for; since long
Autumn has settled down in life for good since long

I have since made the vast desert my permanent abode
Away from the human civilization since long

These dunes on desert are at the mercy of the wind 's velocity
They are forced to change their abode every now and ten

This world of our is full of turmoil and upheavals
Whether be it desert or city or vast oceans

Changing season is sign of eternal change
Change is only permanent rest are transient

This saga of change has been there since
birth of of the universe and shall remain till eternity.

By Mamutty chola

MAGIC OF POSITIVE THOUGHT

When I realised, mistakes lie within me not in others
I regained mental tranquillity, peace at heart and stability in life

News is news nothing bad, nothing good
All depend on your thinking

Time is like a fog
Today is reality, live with vigour

Learning has no age limit
Either for teacher or for student

If you continue to do what you can do
You will remain where you are
How can you excel in life?

Everything is fine, does not mean things are fine
It means your focus is on what is wrong not who is wrong.
By Mamutty chola

Every One Deserves

Every one deserves to be
master of one's destiny

God is merciful, kind benevolent
Success follows after each failure

One door closes another opens
God is all knowing and omniscience

Never sell your faith and soul for money
Wisdom shines supreme, no diamond can match

Freedom in danger is better than liberated slavery
Never trust opportunist and time servers in life

Time is kind and supreme in all situation
Many came and went into oblivion

Never live for self, animals also do
Live for others, giving is sharing

Live life with positivity with joy and fun
Love your life, your life is very lonely

To err is human being progeny of Adam
Never raise fingers at others unless you are perfect.
By Mamutty chola

POWER OF INTEGRITY

When you have nothing to fear and nothing to hide
That is sign of your integrity.

Integrity can only guarantee a bright future in life
nothing else; power, fame and wealth are all transient

Integrity means; come what may, never change one's value

Man of integrity gives equal importance to both small and big matters in life.

A man without integrity can never be trusted.
A burden on self and the society.

Integrity is that force which keeps you on right path
In all situations

Our fame and reputation are what world thing of us,
integrity is what we really are.
By Mamutty chola

MAGIC OF FAILURES

Failures are like milestones in the journey of life
I accept my failures with all humility but
I will not accept defeat and stop trying.

Every successful person had had era of failures
Failures and success are inseparable in life.

Our achievement in life is not in our victory
But overcoming the defeats like phoenix

The beauty of a setback is it gives us opportunity
To try again learning from past mistakes in failures.

We all fail in life who has not failed if we had tried.
The real failure is when you start externalising your failures

To be wrong is nothing because to err is human unless
You live with guilt complex of failure rest of your life.

Give life freedom to fail you will be surprised
To see the astonishing results of your efforts.

By Mamutty chola

FAILURE BUILDS CHARACTER

The winners are never afraid of losing.
Those avoid taking risk are real losers.

In failures are hidden secrets of success.
So never give up, keep the efforts on
Take inspiration from sea waves; never give up

Come to think of there are neither success nor failures
All are nothing but experiences and reactions in life

Nothing is permanent but change so
Neither success or failure but change

Nothing ventures, nothing gains, goes the saying.
In the fast changing world only strategy which
guarantees your failure is not taking risk.

Failure builds character, success takes credit
For that reason, we say nothing succeeds like failure.

The fatal mistakes we all make in life is to be fearful of failure
Remember, fear is a dark room where only negatives are developed.

By Mamutty chola

Jealousy Is Blind

Always treat your failure as an event, not your defeat.

Saga of human civilization say the biggest failure followed the biggest success.

Learn from flower the art of living. It never competes but blooms Next to each other and spreads fragrance .

If you wish to be happy in life, follow two principles
First stop living in the past and second, stop finding faults in others

Whoever wants to see you down are really below you !!
.
Human nature is such all good things about your friends are questioned
and all bad things are believed –it is called jealousy!!!

Never blame the world, whatever happens to you
are direct results of your thought and action in life.

By Mamutty chola

DEPARTED NEVER COMES BACK

Why there is never ending gloom
Happiness disappeared since long
All efforts in vain
Sadness reigns supreme

At times I think
Why not to say goodbye
since soul is immortal
Body is assemblage of earth

Let me go and visit land of unknown
Is that world also having same upheavals?
When death is certain,
then why to fear death

Time flies, autumn came
Caused the leafs to fall
When I looked around
Found trees dressed up like brides

Realised what a tragedy
Youth and time never come back
Unlike season which reminds us
Happiness and sadness are inseparable

If gone time would have come back
We had never been separated
With our loved ones in life
But now they live in our hearts till death.
By Mamutty chola

FAME IS TRANSIENT

Whenever injustice happens,
It is bad omen for the country

World is always busy
In finding faults in others

Have you ever thought
How lonely you are

No time for self and loved ones
Life is not only work
There are other commitments to meet

Whatever you hear is opinion and not facts
Whatever you see is perspectives and not truth

Nature wants us to listen more and talk less
For that reasons we have two ears and one mouth

Beauty is matchless wonder but transient
We can see vision of creator in beauty

Happiness is that moment of life
We all spend it in bliss and joy

Fame is like bouquet presented on achievement
But transient; will wither change being permanent.

By Mamutty chola

LIFE IS A SUSPENSE

What is this life no happiness since years?
All efforts failed, happiness has been elusive

It was only yesterday, Autumn was reigning
All around withered leafs at the mercy of wind

Now with the advent of Spring, greenery every where
Realised, happiness and sorrow are inseparable
Season does come back; alas, gone time never

What a delight it would have been if,
Gone time returns, we had never been
separated with loved ones. It is a reality, loved ones
once depart never come back but their memories do .

At time I wonder why not say goodbye to this world
After all soul is immortal, then why to fear death
Let me visit kingdom of unknown to know mystery of life.
By Mamutty chola

THE CHANGE IS PERMANENT

We cannot change future
But we can prepare ourselves

Only guarantee to success is to change .
Attitude to change is key to change

All changes invite conflict of interests,
Best way to evaluate people's attitude to change .

The people do not object to change
if they are informed why change.

All resistance   change has its genesis in fear.

The change being permanent
Change is inevitable for survival.

Things don't change, they are made to change
To make them relevant to meet the ends.
By Mamutty chola

Faith In God

There is no substitute to faith in God
End result; success in all your efforts

If you wish to help, help not only
humanity but all creation of God.

Faith in self and in God is that power,
Impossible becomes possible,
if you don't trust, try once.

God has gifted us with wisdom
Share it with all, givers are winners

God power is omniscience, you
Need to trust, happiness and sorrow
All come and go passing phase; like season

Never be disappointed in God's benevolence
He is there with you at every steps
You need to have faith in self and God.

Never look for proof of God else where
Presence of soul within you is proof of God.!!
By Mamutty chola

MAY ASIFA SOUL REST IN PEACE

{Inspired by the tragic end of life of 8 years Old CHILD in J&K- VICTIM OF RAPE)

The monsters who raped and killed 8years old child -Asifa
Are not human but products of hatred called Hindutva?

How can they say they are Hindus, one of the most?
Tolerant religions in the world known in the history

The rising intolerance since2014 in the country
Is not rooted in Hinduism but in Hindutva

Unless checked, will turn the country into a volcano
We all must fight and banish the monster called hatred

By spreading true message of Hinduism—
Peace, tolerance, compassion, live and let live

Let us celebrate our unity in diversity
The very message of India's 5000years civilization.

India is not product of one thought or ideology
India is confluence of multi cultures and multi religions

Those who fail to learn from their history
Will be thrown into dust bin of history!!

United we stand divided we fall.

By Mamutty chola

Understand Life

Given the fast changing life, keep your focus on today
Rather living in the past and lamenting on missed opportunities

Every day begins with new hope so live in today
Neither live in the past which is shadow nor in future which is like fog

Trust me what matters is how you have spent your yesterday
And how you have planned to spend today rest will fall in line by default

Do not worry, worry is debt which you do not owe to any one
Never doubt and be a victim of uncertainty in life
Trust and have faith in self the key to success in life

No use of reading holy scriptures, if you do believe in them
The experienced which we gained in life is the best teacher
Self-interest is supreme rest all are transient in life

Never search for that person in life who deserves your love
If any one does deserve your love and care it is you my friend.

By Mamutty chola

A Man With Courage Is Majority

You cannot build your reputation on
Your plans yet to be executed.

Reputation is a responsibility to be kept
To enjoy continued goodwill of the people.

Reputation and fame are external to your
Personality which are outcome of your
achievements in whatever you accomplish.

Without passion nothing can be
achieved in any walk of life.

Passion is that eternal blaze of fire
Very difficult to be extinguished.

One man with passion and courage
always is the majority

Absence of humour makes life barren
Such life will have the echo of grave yard.
By Mamutty chola

BIGGER THE PROBLEM GREATER IS THE SUCCESS.

Yesterday's storm destroyed all the nests on the trees
Oh God, how the birds would spend their night and where

It is better not to learn anything than learning wrong thing
I was standing on the sea shore saw a boat amidst storm

What a similarity with my life ;been struggling since long
Loved ones departure   always remain deep in our hearts

It is wrong to believe once cheated, people forget with passage of time
And the guilty lives with guilt in rest of his life in repentance
Hardly   ever heard, read about or knew any such example in life

Reason, guilty first kills his conscience before committing the crime
When there is no conscience question of repentance does not arise

Never ever there had been any person who was liked by all during his life time
Whether might have been a prophet, saint, king, reformer , scientist, or a poet

All hah had to face adversities; some assassinated, some poisoned and some exiled
Never understood the mysteries of nature's justice why bad things happened to good people

All these fame, wealth, power are transient like fleeting time
Men are helpless when adversities knock at their doors

One thing proved beyond doubt again and again the bigger is the problem
Greater is the success, what is needed is patience, tolerance and perseverance.
By Mamutty chola

Genius Is A Superman In A Man

Only noble souls can be poets
They live in the hearts and minds
of people till eternity; examples
are Rumi, Amir Khusro, Ghalib. Khalil Jibran
Omar Khayyam, Keats, Byron and others

Many achievements are the results
of small ideas like a seed transforming
into a big trees.

For thinking person idleness
is the worst punishment
like solitary confinement,

Rhyme is the soul of poetry, is
all powerful and invincible; can
inspire king and pauper alike.

Sign of wisdom is that the more you
learn the more you feel you are ignorant.

Aim of life is not to achieve something but to
become some one of value to humanity.

Genius is not first among men but
a superman in a man.

Supreme happiness in life is that
realization that you are being loved
for your sake without any ulterior motive
despite your many shortcomings.

Habit formation has to be nurtured
and taken care so that children with
right values are developed for them
betterment and that of society.
As saying goes habit is the nursery
of deviant behaviour.
By Mamutty chola

LET US SAVE MOTHER EARTH

The trees are the poetry of nature on earth
Abode of birds, animals, and numerous insects

Sea waves have always been inspiring humanity to fight on with courage
Sea is abode of fisheries and natural resources for humanity

Rains bring freshness, greenery and rejuvenate lives on earth
Rivers are abodes of all human civilization in the world.
Wind is very source of existence of creatures on earth

Ice covered mountain kissing skies remind us brides in wait besides being fountain head for all rivers.
Clouds are harbingers of happiness to rain- starved land near and far

Moon, stars and galaxy in the solar systems illuminate our lives on earth
Seasonal rainbows add beauty and charm and radiate our lives

Alas despite the benevolence of nature, we human are bent upon destroying mother earth in our greed based craze for development unmindful of danger lurking from behind the oblivious shadow of horizon.

If the madness is not checked, our earth would turn into a fire ball.
Then, beware, we can't eat money

WE ALL MUST SAVE MOTHER EARTH SO THATE WE CAN HANDOVER A BETTER WORLD TO NEXT GENERATION.
Oh men! are you listening?
By Mamutty chola

Trust Is Life

It takes years to build relationship
Does n't take a second to destroy it

Trust is the only basis of durable relationship
If trust is lost everything is lost in life

Trust is like two-wheeled vehicle
Both wheels have to work in unison

If want to win trust of person in life
Win it based on your positive action

If wish to know whether you can trust some one
The best criterion is to trust him by reposing
Faith in him.

The whole human life's happiness rests on trust
Without trust, no relationship is live able.

All broken things can be repaired in life
Except trust, once broken, broken for life

Human tragedies are nothing but saga of loss of trust
Be it love, war, friendship or hatred villain is distrust.
By Mamutty chola

GOD IS OMNIPRESENT

One day my baby doll asked me,
Papa, tell me where is God?
why can't we see him?

I looked at her with smile and admiration
Said I, ho my love, look around

He is everywhere in nature.
Be it sun rise or sun set
Be it Moon , stars, and galaxy
Be it cool morning breeze
Be it mighty sea waves
Be it flow of crystal streams
Be it majestic ice covered Himalaya
Be it rains with its rhythmic sound
Be it dancing leaves on the tall trees
Be it seasons of various hues and colours
Be it enchanting rainbow in the bark clouds
Be it blossoming of buds into flowers
Be it meadows spread miles and miles in the valley
Be it the peacocks strutting by, and deer's acrobats
Be it our loving dog-- Bozo now resting in his heavenly abode
Be it the majestic walk of lions in the forest
Be it birds and falcon flying high in the skies
Be it caravan of royal clouds carrying shades and water far and near
Be it vast deserts and its changing dunes
And be it our soul in our body

God is omnipresent. We can only feel
and experience His presence within us.

How I wished I had a photograph of Him
I would have hung it in our drawing room!!

It is all mater of **faith and believe my love** .
She gave beautiful **smile and said you are a great papa.**
-Mamutty chola

THRILLS OF CHILDHOOD

What is fear? Why do people fear?
Fear is that debt you do not owe
Reason for fear is ignorance.

Believe me you all have only one
Co-traveler in life. And that is you,
And only yourself my friend

One of the key tragedies of our lives is that
we fail to keep pace with time. Result, left behind in life

If someone willingly listens to you what you wish to say,
You will be delighted to share your thoughts with that person
Good listeners are great leaders

The most beautiful thing in our life is truth
There is no substitute to truth. Truth is God

Courage is that spirit in a person which enables
That person to face unforeseen challenges with confidence

Do you know all the major crimes are products of idle minds?
If you don't believe revisit the lives of the dangerous criminals.

A happy childhood is a blessing of God.
Those who grow up without experiencing
the thrills of childhood, will live with
an abyss and vacuum in life.
By Mamutty chola

NATURE'S MIRACLE

If you are determined in life,
All failures can be ladders to success

Look back, saga of human struggles
Are nothing but failures, and success

Deprivation ignites within you the fire
To achieve things first seemed impossible
And make one realise value of those things

Ask a thirsty value of water,
Ask hungry the value of food

Ask the traveler walking in scorching heat
The value of shade and protection

Ask deprived children the **value of happy childhood**
Ask an orphan the value of parent's love
Ask a separated soul the value togetherness

Ask a sad person the value of touching smile
Ask hate, the value of love

Ask broken hearts the value of promises kept
Ask an illiterate the value of education

Ask war the value of peace
Ask old age the value of youth

Ask failure the value of success
Ask a sick man the value of health

Strange are the intents of nature creations
For every thing there are two aspects to it.
By Mamutty chola

TRUST IS FOUDATION OF HUMAN SOCIETY

Trust is that quality which is supreme and
Which acts as glue in strengthing human
Relationships.

Trust is the very foundation of life
A must for in all aspects of human lives.

Trust is soul of human relationship; be it personal,
social or work places. The edifice of human societies
is built on trust, integrity and mutual respects

The genesis of daily saga of break ups in us
relationships, world over is rooted in greed and
self-centred arrogance of I, me and myself.

To start with the seeds of trust have to be sown in
our family values, educational institutions,
and workplaces. This is an evolutionary process
of character building. It is neither available on sale
in the market nor in charity.

There is no substitute to trust, integrity and character
For evolution of ethical based human society.
By Mamutty chola

TRUTH IS ALL POWER

Message of all religious scriptures is peace, love, tolerance
Then why this genocide, and war among the followers of faiths
Life journey is saga of events, success and failures
Rise and fall are natural phenomenon of life
Why do you boast of tolerating others?
Do you know how many are tolerating you in life?
I know the power of truth. Truth is that eternal light
Which shines even in pitch darkness in life
The trees which have deep roots often give sweet fruits
One who is by nature believes in finding faults with others
Are always left behind in life both by loved ones and friends alike
All hates can be won over with power of love
Love is invincible can't be defeated in life.
By Mamutty chola

TIME IS OMNIPOTENT

Time has always remains omnipotent in the world
Those who keep pace with time are always successful
Time is a free treasure one can use any time but
We can't save nor we can keep time in lock and key
Gone time never returns like season; it is a divine mystery
Those who fail to keep pace with time
Are destined to suffer in life always
Time is not only invaluable but power and wealth
Those who spend their today wisely
Their future will take pride in their gone yesterday
It is wrong to presume that you are victims of time
Rather you are victim of your thoughts, and actions
Never blame the world for your failures
Time gives equal opportunity to one and all
Some become Like Barack Obama and some pauper.
By Mamutty chola

FIRST DESERVE

There was a time
I was on top of fame
I am now nobody but my shadow
Ignorance is curse
Soul is starved to death
Education is not only a refuge
But enrichment for soul
It is wrong to think you can change future
Create capabilities within you
Let there be demand for your
Talent everywhere like magnet
Whoever controls situation
Controls direction of his life
Time passes, situation changes
Circumstances are co-travellers of time
Guide you to your destination in life
The lesson I have learned in life
Change being permanent
All success is like a transit camp
So every step is an examination in life!!
By Mamutty chola

DEATH IS CERTAIN

When death is definite why to fear death
After death we are not there then why to worry
When no one has ever escaped death, how can we?
Death is not the end of life
We would all meet on the day of   judgement
Say Quran, Bible, and Torah to their faithful
Gita says life and death is an ongoing events
Soul being immortal, why to fear death
If you wish to earn immortality after you are gone
Try to live in people 's heart, we all live in our homes
Live life like road, has no destination of its own
But help all to reach their destination in life!!
By Mamutty chola

Reflections

If friendship is your weakness
Then you are a noble soul on earth

There was no shade in the long
Journey of life, I took shelter
Under my own shadow in life

How I wished, I had a beloved like mirror
And enjoyed happiness and sorrow together in life

In love broken heart does not mean end of love
Losers are gainers in love since they keep the love alive

Ho my love, I have no space for self within me,
Since you are omnipresent within me

Never be in search of good man in life
First you become a good man in life

Never break the mirror for your ugly look
Mirror reflects reality without fear and favour.
By Mamutty chola

EVLUTION OF HUMAN SOCIETY

There has come to stay three strata of society
The rich, the middle class and the poor

The rich live in their own world
Unmindful of the sufferings of the deprived
Their focus in life is to earn profit, live king's life
All actions with focus on self-aggrandisement
Be it personal, business or social commitments
No action, if there is no profit in return
For that reason they have been the target
Of all revolutions in regime change

The middle class live with focus
On do and die to meet their aspirations
They take every set back as defeat
Be it on personal, career or social fronts
They decide values in society and
Act as custodian of cultural heritage
They are harbingers all changes in society
Be it regime change or cultural change
The government of the day try their best
To treat the middle class as barometer
Of public opinions and respect their sentiments

The oppressed class is the backbone of any society
They are the foot soldiers to transforms government
Plans into reality but have been subject of exploitation
In all ages down the human civilization under all regimes

They lead a hand to mouth existence under all
Types of regimes; be it democracy, communism, autocracy
The power that be used them to capture power
Once in power, exploit them to remain in power.

No country can become developed and prosperous
Unless all the three segments work in union for
inclusive development. Failing which social turmoil
will be the common feature in any society world over.

By Mamutty chola

Message Of Wisdom

*A*cts of kindness is better than any forms of prayers

Slips of tongue is more dangerous than slips of steps

*Ill-manner is like a dress which can fit into
anyone without measurement*

*The difference between wise man and fool is that wise man
knows his weakness whereas fools exhibit his weakness
by his ill-advised actions*

*When you are on top of your fame your friends know
who you are and when you are down,
you know who your friends are.*

*Words are under your control till spoken,
once spoken you are under its control said Hazard Ali.*

By Mamutty chola

EVERY DAY IS GIFT OF GOD

The one who celebrates every day as gift of God
Is wise as compared to one who mourns over
Each passing day as lost opportunity in life.

I feel enthralled whenever I visit sea shore
And witness mighty musical sea waves.
The echo of sea waves remind me of harmonized
Rhythms from the nature's piano par excellence.

The city of Mumbai India's commercial capital
Has hidden in its womb the beautiful sea beaches,
 Romantic rain, High rise building ,its life giving
Local/metro rails, Mumbai never sleeps, abode
Of humanity from across the globe. Inhabitants
Young and old, children and woman all on move
On24by 7 in search of their dreams with vigour, joy
and hopes for better future. Her heart is very big
Ever ready to welcome all. A true cosmopolitan city
with her airports and Bollywood of international
repute and fame.

Human thoughts, and feelings when oppressed
and suppressed, give birth to anger , hate and
Revulsion waiting to explode in tears. When
Find a sympathetic soul ready to hear with concerns,
Can salvage the sufferings. If not heard may result
In revolution and regime change. Suppression and
Oppression is the worst form of injustice. Says saga
of human civilization down the ages.
By Mmutty chola

JOURNEY OF EXCELLENCE

Determination to seek truth is more
important than will to believe in truth.

Wisdom being the sum total of our experience
When applied in solving human issues. has always
Been a success in all situation without exception.

Music and human soul have deep connection
For that reason, the best company of solitude.

Success and failure are two sides of a coin
Like all creations have two side; day and night
Life and death. Even nature has created all
creatures in pairs.

All dejected souls love Autumn more than spring
They see their reflections in the autumn leaves
Scattered and crushed all around unlike flowers
In full bloom being darling of lovers of all ages.

All human efforts to achieve perfection shall remain
An incomplete dream because perfection is beyond
human reach. Excellence yes, but not perfection,
Perfection is an attribute attributable to nature.
For that reason, excellence is a journey and not a
Destination. Change being permanent, all success
are transient. Journey of excellence is never ending till eternity.
By Mamutty chola

FALL FROM FAULTLESS TO FAULT

Fall from faultless to fault takes a split of second
but the reverse journey takes a life time.

When we look around there is romance and music
Even divine scriptures are in poetry be it Quran
 Gita, Bible, or Torah. It goes to proof that God is the
The perfect poet among all poets; unmatched .

Success and gain, however small and insignificant
Are indeed success and gain. A matter of joy and celebration

In life reach is important but grasp is ultimate motto.

A moment fall from grace becomes a cause for repentance for life

When the journey of life, if ridden with ups and down, rise and fall
High and low, success makes you forget pains of struggles.
Like a painful dreams. The thrills of struggles are
always inspiring, motivating and challenging in life.
By Mamutty chola

DYNAMICS OF THOUGHTS AND ACTIONS

Life stares at me like a question mark
It has been ages since happiness
Migrated to land of unknown.

Morning comes and evening comes
Time is flowing non-stop unchecked.
Many seasons came and went.

Alas autumn has been my companion since long
When I glance at fallen leaves scattered all over
At the mercy of wind like kites cut off
and blown up in the sky In the wind .

Autumn means withering of leaves as harbinger
of spring. All trees bloom with greenery all around
In spring. Birds of all types sing songs in praise
of nature welcoming the advent of spring

Strange are ways of the nature. Our lives are like seasons
Happiness and sorrow, joy and cry, tears and smiles
Change is permanent. Alas! seasons do come back
but not gone time

Time has a permanent companion in circumstances as
Perennial co-traveler. If handled wisely, that decides
our destiny while our sojourn on earth. What matters is
our feelings, thoughts and actions.

True, in life right thinking is the arbiter of our lives
So keep your thought above prejudice, and fear
Success will be yours   my friend in life.
By Amity chola

Life Is A Sojourn On Earth

Our life is a sojourn on earth
It is up to us how to live.
Those who control circumstances
Control their lives. Those who fail
Disappear into oblivion unsung.

Nobody plays this life with marked cards
Your success and failure depend on
Positive thoughts and focused actions.

This life of ours is meaningless, if we
Don't have someone to share our
Feelings with since God has created all
creatures in pairs.

Love unites humanity and universe
Because love is immortal like soul.

In life when relationship becomes
A burden, you must be brave enough
To say enough is enough. Lady luck will
Reward you with smile.

Always remember, reward of your life
Is not what you have achieved in life but
What you have become in life.

Trust me you will never be able to achieve
any thing in life, if you are afraid of fear of
Failure.Fear is a darkroom where only negatives
are developed.

In life we all act as per our scripts inherited
In our genes. If scripts are positive,
then we are a success else a failure in life.

An inquisitive mind finds opportunities
in all situations. Hallmarks of all achievers in life.
By Mamutty chola

An Utopian Dream

All these talks of equality have no reality
Even nature does not believe in equality
Except in death!!!

All laws are enacted for law breakers
Not for law abiding citizens

In real life democracy is not for the people
But a means for politicians to perpetuate
themselves in power.

For saying sake, country belongs to people
But in reality in democracy we are liberated
Slaves bogged down under never ending
Restrictions claiming to be for our benefits.

No success is worth celebration, if achieved
By following unethical means. You may gain
world but lose your soul!!!

There is no substitute to wisdom because
It is the sum total of our experience in life.

The flow of time is non stoppable
Neither can be stored as wealth
But more powerful than power and wealth.

I have a vision of a world where humanity living in peace.
But alas, it will ever remain an utopian dream. Men being
homo sapiens have a tendency to dominate over
others based on creed, caste, colour and religion.
Human civilization of Trillian years are a testimony
To the wars, genocides and self-destruction since beginning.

By Mamutty chola.,

Time And Circumstances

There is deep connection between time and circumstances
Like relation between sea and sea waves

Nothing to match speed of time always on move
Time and circumstances are like a co-travellers

Circumstances take birth from the womb of time
Remain together like inseparable soul always

Same is the relation between sea and sea waves
Waves have no existence of its own without sea

There is message for humanity to follow
Whoever adapts to the changing reality

Is key to success since change is permanent
When it comes to goal in life, all goals are transient

Here pro-activeness and focused vision are essential
For guaranteed success each and every time

All creatures are in pairs; a miracle of nature
So is the case with time and circumstances.
By Mamuttychola

POWER OF IMAGINATION

Human advancement is attributable
To imagination. It inspires us to dream,
Hope, and be positive in life. So all
inventions, innovations and creativity
Originate from the womb of imagination.
Imagination is like wings to falcon which
Enables it to fly high in the sky beyond horizon,

Key to ignorance is knowledge,
Wisdom is the name of experience
We gain wisdom not by reading books
 but by experience.! !!

No pain, no gain. Sweetest memories
are those that remind us of our struggles.
And its life giving melodies of all time.

Each change in life ushers in new
Challenge in life. Since time and
circumstances are co-travellers.
Capable conquer new frontiers.
Incompetent disappear into
Oblivion; unsung.

Meeting of souls of separated
Lovers either while alive or after death
Are the culmination of true love.

Soul being immortal is beyond
The realm of death.

While alive we dislike, hate, conspire
Feel jealous of each other but in
Death we unite to celebrate
the good deeds of the departed .
Hate only divides and love unites.

By Mamutty chola

NATURE BELIEVES IN CHANGE

Law of nature postulates that all
Small things; be it human or non-human
Either submerge or merge with
Big things like fountains in rivers
Rovers with sea, sea with oceans,
Sorrow with happiness, life with
Death, day with night, hate with
Love. Reverse never happens!!!

Poets, philosophers and scientists
Are gifted with exceptional qualities of foresights
To fathom the unfathomable events hidden
In the womb of time. Be it today's blasphemy
Into tomorrow's truth. Case is point is Galileo's
Discovery that earth rotates around the sun
And not the other way around.

Disappointments, and setbacks in
Any forms must be taken as lesson
To improve one's performance ,
If learned from the mistakes, nothing
Succeeds like failures.

Tears   are with us always in joy and sorrow
A permanent co-travellers from womb to tomb,
Joy lost is always a pain but there is no gain
Without pain says wisdom down the ages.

Music is a song of nature. Hence permeates
All aspects of living beings on earth, be it
Human, birds, animals or insects.
Forest is poetry of nature on earth.

Buds bloom in the gardens, autumn is
The harbinger of spring, rain rejuvenates
Earth with greenery all around and birds
Sing songs of joy in praise of nature.
Message is change is permanent rest
Are transient; be it success, fame or sorrow.
By Mamutty chola

LIVE LIKE MIRROR

Poetry mirrors human lives
With transparency without
Impurity like mirror which stands
For truth, only truth and nothing but truth.

Come what may one must live and
Die like mirror.Even after broken into pieces,
Never loses its character but emerges in
Pieces by retaining its original character.

At times I think if God is benevolent
and merciful why to fear him.
If HE is omnipresent why to search
for Him elsewhere but within us.!

Sorrow and happiness are integral
Part of our lives; human existence.
No escape still alive to complete
Our sojourn on earth.

Time and circumstances, if managed
with foresight will guarantee
A life of bliss, happiness, joy.
Again all rest on your thoughts,
You are what your thoughts are!!

Men being homo sapiens live with

An insatiable urge and desire to
Dominate over others. The very genesis
Of all crime, genocide and war since
Dawn of human civilization on mother earth.
By Mamutty chola

VOICE OF SANITY

Destruction comes before construction.
All chaos ultimately lead to better tomorrow
That has been the saga of human civilization.

Agents of hate of all kinds love martyrdom of fame.
They represent the worst kind of human nature. For
That reasons all divine scriptures describe hate as crime
against humanity.

The people who acquire ill-gotten fame by using
Unethical means must remember that they may rise faster
Than dust, straw and feather and sooner than later
They fall from the top like pack of cards.

The lasting friendship is always based of principles
of equality in all forms unlike love which is based on
Unconditional mutual surrender. Love lasts for ever
When based on principles of friendship.

If anyone has love , feelings and passion for self
And nature, certainly he will be empathetic to the feelings
Of fellow human being.

True love never nurtures ill-will. Even in separation
wishes best for each other since loves unites unlike
hate which divides.
By Mamutty chola

I Am Time

Since the formation of universe
I have been witness to the evolution
Be it humans, animal, birds, nature

Me and circumstances have been
Part of every creature on earth since then
All have been given equal opportunity to excel
Human civilization is nothing but events.

All are equal before me without exception
Be it king, pauper, rich and, oppressed
I have seen the era of ignorance and darkness.

I have been a co-travellers of all prophets, saints
Philosophers, poets, thinkers, be it Moses   David,
Jesus, Mohammed, Ram, guru Nanak, Aristotle,
Socrates ,Alexander Galileo, Ashoka, Akbar. Gandhi
Abraham Lincoln, Nehru, Confucius, Rumi, Ghalib
And others down the ages and their messages to humanity

I have been witness to reign of terror of Halaku, chengez
Khan, Hitler, Mosouloni, Pharaoh, Nadir shah and Nero

It was my misfortune to witness crucifixion of Jesus,
poisoning of Aristotle, Socrates, assassinations of
Abraham Lincoln, Mahatma Gandhi, Indira Gandhi,
Rajiv Gandhi, Martin Luther King jr and President

JF Kennedy.And house arrest of Gallelio till death
for telling truth that earth rotates around the sun
and not other way around.Then considered as blasphemy

Despite knowing war has never brought peace
on mother earth still trillions of human beings
sacrificed at the altar of nationalism, patriotism
for wealth, women and for reason of power and
Intolerance whereas all religion's message is for

peace and peace only.What an irony , I found
human beings always on the path of intolerance
being homo sapiens.I am sad at heart seeing
the increasing trust deficit among men

There is break down in family values, lack of
concerns and care for fellow humans.
I was fortunate to witness undying love of
lovers who laid their lives for their beloveds.
Lovers like Romeo Juliet, LailaMajni Sheri Farhad,
Wamik Azra, and Soni and King Edward of Uk
Who renounced his throne for his love a commoner
They would and will live on till eternity and would be
an inspiration for people of all generation to come.

I enjoy bliss of spring, rain and winter and also share
the sorrow of autumn knowing it is harbinger of
spring .I rejoice mighty waves , morning breeze,
romantic moonlight, shining stars, , ice covered
mountains, flow of crystal clear streams, songs
of birds, musical rain, lush green meadows
I have witnessed the rise and fall of great human
civilization down the ages including great empires

and recent advancement in the fields of science
and technology on unprecedented scales.
The wonder of men landing on the moon and
their endeavours to settle on planets beyond stars.

I am indeed sad and worried for human race
since in their greed for development they are
destroying the mother earth. If the present
phase of destruction not checked, the mother
earth will turn into fire boll. Then men cannot eat money!!

I am time not only powerful and resourceful
but final arbiter of human destiny. Whomsoever
had made good use of me have been successful in life.
CIRCUMSTANCES AND ME WILL DECIDE FATE OF ALL
CREATURES ON EARTH. SO KEEP PACE WITH US ELSE
WILL PERISH INTO OBLIVION UNSUNG!!EVERYTHING
ON THIS EARTH IS WITHIN MY POWER. SO LISTEN TO
THE VOICE REASON; OH MEN!!!
By Mamuty chola

Aim For Better World

Never rest and base your happiness on such things
Attainment of which not only difficult but impossible

My friend, if your intentions are honest
There is no age bar for doing good things

Right path may lead you to your cherished destination
If you choose wrong path, you end up in failure

Yesterday is dead past, remember always
Today is reality, so live in today, key
to future success is hidden in today

Lesson of life, for acts   of kindness
Can always be done without money

Real progress means protection of environment
So that we can hand over a better world to next
generation

Everything rests on your positive thinking
So keep your thoughts positive; key to success in life.

By Mamuty chola

ALL FAME TRANSIENT

If you wish to live a happy life,
live with your loved ones.
Never indulge in rat's race
For amassing wealth and fame
Which are transient like floating clouds.

Invent qualities within you to excel
In life to share happiness with loved ones.
Life is meant to be lived for self and for
loved ones. Once you love self, you would love
the whole world. Love vibrates and unites
unknown souls.
Always creates relevant capabilities and
Right attitudes in self then all impossible
will become possible for you in life.
Never wait for permission from others,
Do what you wish to do but listen to all.
In the matter of hard decision, always
listen to mind and not heart. All major.
follies in life have its genesis in emotional
Decisions.
Ignore world's criticism if you wish to succeed
in life. If you do not believe me, do sit back
And reflect on the lives of great souls of
By gone era; be it prophets, philosopher, thinkers
All had had to face baseless criticism including
death, banishment from home land and life

Imprisonment for speaking the truth then considered as blasphemy. If you wish to be remembered even after you are gone, live in people's hearts now.
By Mamutty chola

Deserving Gets Rewards, Needy Charity

There has never been dearth of appreciators
Yes, indeed there have been dearth of deserving

Demand is always for deserving and not for needy
Deserving gets rewards, needy gets charity in life

I wish to share sign of sad people in life
They smile a lot but carry tsunami within

Friends should be like mirror and shadow
Mirror always tells truth and shadow never leaves you

If you are determined to follow path of honesty
Definitely you journey of life will always be lonely

If our intentions are visible on our faces
Then we will find every one wearing veil

By nature, I help all in life without motives
Friends think I am idle and no definite mission in life!!

Nothing can match the quality of givers
Those who give are always gainers in life

Though death is considered cruel being definite
But she keeps reminding you of good qualities of departed!!!

By Mamutty chola

Relation Between Thought and Action

What an irony, thoughts being the very basis
of our actions are always treated as second fiddle
Actions take all credits and laurels under the sun.

Always remember, problems are an opportunities
to excel and conquer new frontiers in life.
In life treat hopes as your perennial co-travellers
since hope creates future. Hope is a waking dream.
Create capabilities in life, you always be in demand.

You can always count number of seeds in an apple
but you can't guess, how many apples be there
from one seed. This wonder of the nature is beyond
Man's genius Similarly , presence of soul.
within body is the proof of God's existence

Setbacks in life never means you are a failure
Set backs are like ladders to success provided
you learn from past set backs. So we say
nothing succeeds like failures in life.

By Mamutty chola

Have A Look Around

If you curse your fate being
Unfortunate in life, then my friend,
Take a look around then you realize
There are untold millions worse than you

Some are extremely poor,
some extremely sick,
And some are disabled
Still some are bed-ridden

If you are victim of loneliness
Think of those million souls
You must have seen many of
 Them on sea shore, or rly plate form

Your desire to live in palaces
while staying in slum or huts
without resources is a wishful.
thinking .Just think of those
born on foot path or living
under flyover in inhuman conditions

The irony is that even God
 does not believe in equality
Some are born ugly some handsome
Some are very healthy, some very sick

Some are physically fit some disabled
Even five fingers are not equal
Men are born free but are not
Equal in mental and in intellectual
Attributes, temperament and thinking

So create capabilities to be deserving
Needy always live on charity
Our constitution guarantees equal
Opportunity to one and all and not equality.

If you are born poor
It is not your fault but
If you die as poor it's your fault
Learn the lessons of life from
ants and falcon and sea waves
All the three never give up in life.
By Mamutty chola

Strange Are Ways Of Human Thinking

We all dislike darkness but for darkness
Can we ever enjoy the beauty of moonlight?
stars in the galaxy in the sky!
We all lament arrival of autumn how ignorant
we are. Autumn is the harbinger of spring!!
We all dislike and hate deceit and falsehood
But for the evils, we would not have realized
The importance of truth and trust!!
We all condemn enmity but for it, we would
Not have realized the importance of friendship!
We all always mourn failures but for it, we would
Not have tasted the joy of success and victory!
We all hate unfaithfulness but for it we would not
Have realized the importance of faithfulness and loyalty
In love, friendship and relationships.
We all fear death 24 by 7 in life but for death we would not
Have realized the value of human life and our loved ones in life!
We all suffer loneliness in solitude but for it we would not
Have realized the importance of memories; the perennial
companion in loneliness and solitude.
There are two- side to all creation in the world
That is reality and only reality like change in life.
By Mamutty chola

REAP AS YOU SOW

By sowing cactus don't expect roses
By spreading hatred don't expect love
By creating animosity don't expect friendship
By causing hurt you don't expect smiles
By indulging in destruction don't expect Prosperity
By causing death don't exppect life
By indulging in meaness don't expect decency
By raising war don't expect peace
By encouraging injustice don't ever expect justice
By doing unethical one can't become ethical
By reading one can become knowledgeable not wise
By experience only one can become wise.
BY distrusting you can't beget trust; trust only begets trust
Remember always truth and character are invincible.
So we reap as we sow is the divine message.
By Mamutty chola

DON'T BE A PRISONER OF LONELINESS

This life imprisonment of loneliness seems never ending
Even my memories are fading and failing me. My patience
and silence are worried seeing my plights. Oh life tell me
what to do with never ending loneliness in my life

When asked sea waves; my perennial inspiration in life,
Came the reply from within me, oh man get out of self-made
Delusion I have invented.; life means action and positivity;
A must for living with smiles. Embrace life with all its
shortcomings, Failures, joy, sorrow ups and downs, defeats
and victories;
Two sides of life. If we don't change; will become of victims of
Change and will be left alone like lost traveler in vast desert of life.

Try to live like seasons; Autumn is the harbinger of Spring!!
Your best friend and enemy is your feelings, thoughts and actions
Your best asset is you yourself. You do not exist for the world
World exists for you and because of you. Don't you realize how
Neglected and lonely you are, advised the voice of conscience
which is chamber of justice, says Quran.

Live in today. Today is reality, yesterday is dead and a shadow.
World respects victors and not vanquished, Keep pace.
You are what your feelings, thoughts and action are.
Never blame gravity for your fall in life. Thinking
makes all the difference. some become Gandhi and some
Hitler!!
By Mamutty Chola

TOUGH TIME NEVER LASTS

We achieve patience after setbacks in life.
And satisfaction after gaining desired status in life.

Feelings, thoughts and ideas are the genesis of all our actions but alas all praise Credits and laurels go to actions and not to the thoughts and ideas.

In life broken souls never get solace neither in mosque, temple nor in church
what they get in bars are of empathy, fellow feelings, care and concerns in each other company free from all prejudices.

Having taken birth we all have to live our pre-destined scripts be a king, a commoner while our sojourn on earth..so why to grieve, live in today with smile. Who has seen Future, Today is reality.

Life is neither a puzzle nor a dream. Life is nothing but your feelings, thoughts and actions.

One suggestion to one and all, treat less fortunate with love and empathy who knows they will be what you are today in the years ahead.

Do you know whom you dream in your dreams they are none other than your loved ones and part of your inseparable destiny.

Never keep complaining about your loved ones lest you will be left alone!

Ups and downs are part of life. Never break up relations tough time never lasts
Beauty of time live like seasons Autumn is harbinger of spring!!!.
By Mamutty Chola

Food For Thoughts

Only those who remain successful all the times in life are the ones whose vision is focused miles ahead of their immediate goals like falcon.

The biggest victory in life is to conquer self. Know thyself is key to excellence in life

My suggestion to all, never enter into an argument with a person whose opinion has no relevance in your life.

To accept something without understanding is nothing but madness and not to accept a thing without understanding is share foolishness.

Memories neither die nor fade away but remain part of our lives as solace/inspiration both in loneliness and happiness .

One biggest lesson of life is all relations are transient except your self interest!!

Meet always with smiles whomsoever you meet .Life is so uncertain not even a single moment is within Your control.

This heart of ours is amazing. Within it resides love and hate in peace.

These talks of love, loyalty and the promise of life together till death do us part are like floating Clouds at the mercy of velocity of wind. No one dies of broken heart for failure in love. Remember always if you live always in memory of lost love, you will be left alone. Live life and be faithful to one who is your companion in life.

I fail to fathom the intolerance on religious ground when God is one and message of all religions is love, harmony tolerance, humanism and live and let live.

By Mamutty chola

MY HOMAGE TO OUR BELOVED ATALJI

A great visionary, a poet and a statesman of eminence, was Atalji
A person of sterling qualities steeped in humanism and a personification of Indian ethos and values enshrined in our great constitution. Being a wonderful human being, he could get along with all, and always believed and practiced that political disagreement must not affect personal relations.
He was above caste, religion sects and regional bias
Rightly Nehru ji way back in 1957 had predicted that one day Atali would become Prime Minister of India.
Despite ideological differences and upbringings Atalji was more a Nehruvian than a hard core RSS BHAKT!!!. He always believed in uniting people. His focus was always what is wrong instead of who is wrong. His political mantras were love, tolerance and humanism
The unprecedented echo of sorrow and grieve on his passing away from across the nation and political leaders is the biggest tribute to the People Prime Minister
called Atal Bihari Vajpayee.

He will remain a shining star in the galaxy of National leaders who had made India a great country. May his soul rest in peace in his heavenly abode.
By Mamutty Chola

DOES GOD LISTEN TO ALL?

The extreme of love is hate.
Time passes differences widen
Gap between happiness and sorrow is very narrow
Like difference between light and darkness
There is no substitute to justice
If there is any that is injustice
Wisdom has the quality to differentiate
The difference between truth and untruth
It is unwise to depend on others
What you can achieve by yourself
Often found person satisfied in life
Lead a happy life with loved ones.
If God listens and would answer all prayers
Neither there would be enemies or poverty on earth.
Remember, God is within you
You are the creator of your destiny.
By Mamutty chola

What Is Faith?

However long the night be, dawn does follow
your faith can move the mountain and your doubt
Will be a bigger hurdle than a mountain
Faith is fountainhead of hope .Faith does create miracles
Wherever love resides, hate vanishes
All challenges are not hurdles but gateway to success
No power is as great as that of faith and patience
No hurdle can overcome you if you have faith in self
Seen often things achieved with ease are often lost.
Remember always, genesis of all evils is greed.
By Mamutty chola

SECRETS OF HAPPINESS

Ever since I decided to love self, a realization has since dawn
How ignorant was I, totally unware of loneliness of self in life.
Like a fool I was in search of happiness outside instead of within me Focus in life has to be on inventing self, instead of searching self

Seen often, those who love themselves, are the one who loves life
And lead a happy life since sharing is gaining and growing
Givers are always the gainers in life. The biggest secret of life
Known to humanity. Have a look at saga of human civilization
Then you would realize the infinite magic of sharing and growing.

One experience of mine, when you get up in the morning
Dedicate the day as gift to self and look into mirror and greet self
With smile. your self will feel elevated and recognized.
Sadness and gloom will disappear and positivity will reign

Remember, within you there are multiple personalities;
Like of son, husband, brother, father , friend and a boss too
Never allow these personalities overshadow your individual self!!!
Maintain a balance a pre requisite for self-happiness in life
Oh man, your biggest asset of your life is you and you only
Also remember, this world exists for you and for you only
You don't exit for the world.!!!
By Mamutty Chola

MAGIC OF LANGUAGE IS INFINITE

The most powerful thing after time is language.
You can conquer the whole world without a single shot being fired. The language is the biggest unifying and destructive force on earth more powerful than nuclear bomb!!
Without language mother earth would have been a vast, empty desert.
It has the power to turn heaven into hell and vice versa. Human civilization has been a saga of success, defeat, war, peace, progress, all have its genesis in in the usage of language by those who Controlled the destiny of human life on earth?
The prophets, philosophers, Reformers and political leaders who used the language wisely left a mark on the Canvas of time for posterity since ages and those despots who used it for self-aggrandizement left behind signs of destructions all around in human history. Language is the final arbiter in defining beauty of humans and nature both.
The legacy of Aristotle, Socrate, Rumi, Mahatma Gandhi, Nehru, Nelson Mandela, Martin Luther JR, Umar Khayyam, Ghalib, Keats, Baron, Khalil Gibran, Amirkhushro, Galileo, words worth and others could become possible through the medium of language

Do you know the seeds of human civilization were sown when for the first time man used language and not force to register his protest against injustice, the magic of language is indeed infinite.

By Mamutty chola

GENESIS OF CULTURE IS IN SMILE

Never be afraid of falling in love. Life is
meaningless without love.
But never be a sentimental fool to sacrifice
everything for love knowing in life every
thing is transient and subject to change except
self interest.
Precaution is prerequisite at every step in life
But beware, too much of it will be a tragedy
you will become Hamlet in life by becoming a
victim of procrastination;
«TO DO OR NOT TO DO» !!!

I am neither agnostic nor atheist but a firm
believer in God. Because existence of soul within
our body is proof of God.

Crushed and suppressed desires and hopes never
die but remain dormant deep down in our existence
like hidden volcano. A motivation to keep struggles on in life

It is a fact that human culture has its genesis in smile.
It originated first time when man used words to express
His anger instead of violence.

Women are a great mystery.No one till date could discover
What actually are their desires, Even Adam after losing paradise
for Eve, still search is on!!!

Music is spiritual companion of humanity on earth.
Oh man! do not issue fatwa/dictate against music.
You must know all the religious scriptures be it;
Quran, Gita, Bible, Tohra and Guru Grant Saheb
are revealed in musical poetry!!
By Mamutty chola !

LIFE MEANS STRUGGLES

Oh God! Why this life is a never ending ups and downs.
What childhood, what youth or what twilight of my
life, I remain thirsty despite residing on river side.

Misfortunes have been my life companions since long.
Life has been like kite cut off from string and floating in
the sky at the mercy of velocity of the stormy wind.
Worst still I feel lost all alone in in vast desert amidst
changing shifting dunes since ages.

Many seasons came and went by   but Autumn has been
my perennial companion in life. Even pleasant memories of the
Good days have since become dim like a distant dream

Come what may, I am determined to rise like phoenix and
achieve lost glory and status once again and restore the
lost smiles of my loved ones before I complete my sojourn
on mother earth.
By Mamutty chola

Journey Of Life

Happiness and sorrow, life and death
Are perennial companions of life while alive
One who understood the designs of nature
Could lead a happy and balanced life while alive
One who fails to fathom the designs of God
Is certain to live a marooned life while alive.
While our sojourn one earth every one of us
without exception has to pass through these
phases. Being creation of nature these ups
and downs are prescripted in our genes.
By Mamutty chola

Man And Nature

What does man possess?
Since birth to death?
Always depends on others
Parents give birth to him
Parents bring him up
Parents and teachers educate him
Works entire life for others
He marries also others
Even lives in memories of others
On death others cremate him
Comes to the world empty hands
Departs from the world empty hands
Nothing man owns but being a care taker while alive
Man is puppet in the hands of nature
Secret of our existence while on earth
Dependability is key to our existence.
Man can do nothing alone except in bathroom while alive !!!
Be an emperor, despot, or Prime minister !!
Alas! Oh man then why this I, ME AND MYSELF ego trips.
By Mamutty chola

SIMPLICTY, TOLERANCE AND KINDNESS

Denial of justice is always injustice
Revolution has been the consequences
In all stages of human civilization down the ages
To bring unprecedented changes in society.

when the revolt for change fail, it is called mutiny
Our fight for freedom in 1857 is the historical example of mutiny.

Never bother about others opinions in life
If you don't wish to be prisoner of other thoughts

There are three human qualities; very crucial in life
They are simplicity, tolerance and kindness

Person gifted with such refined attributes
Not only live for self but live for whole humanity

Those who overpower others, are powerful
But those who have self-confidence are master
of their own destiny

A house is comprised of doors, windows, walls and roofs
The space within is called home with loved ones.
By Mamutty chola

What Is Disappointment?

When you give up in life
When you think you can't do anything
When you thing nothing is within your power
When all your efforts fail in life
When loved ones desert you
When whom you trusted betrayed you
When best friends turn enemies
When your guide become predator
When you experience betrayal and mistrust
When you think life is burden
When you lose confidence in self
When you always talk of past failures
When you love your loneliness
When you always live in the past
When you convince self, life is not worth living
When you feel like committing suicide
These negatives thoughts are recipe for
Self-destruction in life
Never allow such thoughts dominate you
Nothing succeeds like failure provided you learn from mistakes
Life is a gift of nature. Live it with joy
Live in today, Tomorrow never comes
Think positive you are nothing but your thoughts!!!
By Mamutty chola

DEATH IS CERTAIN WHY TO FEAR

All say death is a curse, when death is
Certain why to blame death for nothing.

Never once death has failed in her commitment
Since dawn of life on mother earth.

Her loyalty is unmatched and unparalleled
Once she comes takes along her chosen one

We human are very hypocrite, While alive life
Gives us so much troubles still we love our life

Death just for performing her divine mission is
Blamed for nothing. Fear of death is like a dark room

Abode of negativity. So why to worry when alive
When you are dead how does it matter, my friend!!!.

One beauty of death is, she turns the departed soul
Into an embodiment of virtues. We all talk good of
departed soul and pray for his/her well being in heavenly abode.

That day is not far may be 30-40 years down the line
we, human can prolong our stay on mother earth not
only 100 years but 200-300 years or even immortality
with the help of Artificial intelligence I!!! It is not a fantasy
Yesterday's fantasy is today's reality. Do you agree?
By Mamutty chola

Right Thinking

When I was young,
Mother would advice
Never worry, worry
WILL age you faster
Now I understand, worry is
A curse worse than poison

Learn to live in people's hearts,
We all live in our homes
Like wind, we can't see time
But time keeps track of all
While we are alive

Death of feelings means
Death of conscience such
Death we don't hear.
Never blame love, love is God
Love is neither true or false
It is we the human who are
Either truthful or untruthful

Did you ever realize
Why some people prosper
and some wither away in crisis
Reasons their thinking

In life our feelings, thoughts
And actions are the final arbiter
of our destiny.so we say you are
What your thoughts are
Never blame gravity for you fall!!
By Mamautty choli

JOURNEY OF HONESTY IS ALWAYS LONELY,

There has never been any dearth of needy in the world
In fact there has been dearth of deserving all the time

If you are keen to know signs of sad people in life
Mark those who smile all the time in all situations

If you are looking for dependable friend in life
Choose one who has the qualities of mirror and shadow
For mirror always speaks truth and your shadow never leaves you

If you have to choose a path of honesty, then my friend
Be prepared for a lonely journey while your sojourn on earth
The road to honesty is never crowded unlike dishonesty!!

Tolerance is that quality which is exceptional and unmatched
Tolerance never fails you; come what may in your struggle in life

our face being index of mind, if intentions are visible on our face, no wonder we will find every one wearing veils to hide their real self.

Giving and sharing are sterling human qualities in life
In real life givers have been the biggest gainers in life

No doubt death does snatch away our loved ones from us. But she keeps reminding us of the caring and loving qualities of the the departed souls till we are alive.
By Mamutty chola

WHY TO ACT AS BLIND?

Hopes creates future
Hope and self confidence
Are essential for success
In life in all spheres of life

Have ever thoughts the
most beautiful moments
Of your life? The moments
Spent with your loved ones

Success of year's efforts make
You forget sufferings undergone
Like advent of spring after autumn
Life means change which is permanent

Life without love is like
Withered garden without life
When love reigns our life
Life becomes ever green meadow

I pity those unfortunate souls
Despite having vision still
Behave like men without
Vision and refuse to enjoy life

Nothing ventures, nothing gains
Goes the saying. Happiness neither
Falls from heaven nor you get in
Charity.First deserves, then desires!

Whenever we raise cry of war
It does cause seamless destruction
Whenever we talk of peace it
Ushers in climate of peace like spring.
By Mamutty Chola

MIRROR DOES NOT REFLECTS TRUTH ALL THE TIME

Always judge a person based on his question
Never based on his answer; yes it is correct

If wish to do justice, do it in favour of deserving
Trust me you will always remain in people's heart

Never think money is the be all and end all in life
Else all decision will be based on money
We can't eat money nor can command passion

It is wrong ;mirror mirrors your true nature
If you wish to know your worth, know how other value you

Knowledge is that ocean depth. of which none could fathom
Be it Socrates, Aristotle, Rumi, Confucius or Buddha!!!

Trust me, poverty is invincible and will remain till eternity
Reasons; those in power never treat their authority as their
Responsibility.Very genesis of poverty among humanity!!!
By Mamutty chola

VOICE OF REASON

A society which can't prevent injustice
Is sure to disappeare into oblivion sonner or later

What a pass we all have come in our life ,
There is no restriction on nightingale singing

But there are restrictions every where
on human thoughts and speeches!

Happiness has no meaning without dignity
Freedom with danger is better than be a liberated slave

Death of negative thoughts is the genesis
For the birth of new ideas in society

If there exists no restriction on injustice in society
Then laws of jungle shall prevail seamlessly in society
Those who fail to keep pace with time will perish

Wisdom we gain from experience and knowledge
From reading and interacting with others. For that reason
Knowledge speaks and wisdom listens!!

Being human; our source of happiness differs
from person to person. For that reasons, no two
persons are alike. Even if born to same parents
and living under the same roof and sky!
By Mamutty chola

BUSYNESS AND LONELINESS

When injustice happens in society
It is a sign of death of humanism

Famous and honest are always in demand
But there are more people jealous than envious of them!!

Do you ever ponder; your busyness has made
You and your loved ones how lonely in life

Did you ever ask yourself and your loved?
Ones? How lonely they are in their lives .
Remember life is not only work in life
There are other commitments to redeem in life

Do remember whatever we hear is an opinion
and not truth and whatever we see is not
A reality but a perspective; a point of view.

Nature has created us to listen and see more
For that reasons we have two ears and two eyes

Beauty is enchanting but transient like rainbow
In real beauty we see images of creator

Happiness is that bliss in life
we share with loved ones in life

Fame is like a bouquet presented on victory
Alas both are like bubbles on the water!!!

By Mamutty chola

Curse Of Poverty

The biggest enemy of humanity has been the poverty
In all stages of human civilization rulers have been exploiting
the poor by selling them dreams since time immemorable.

No country in the world is immune to poverty and exploitation
The slogan remove poverty was used as opium to fool the ruled
The poverty as curse has been ruling the world as unfettered
and invincible Evil on earth.

Many isms like communism, socialism and capitalism came
to power to remove /eradicate poverty but all have turned
into predators instead of saviour of humanity.

As long as greed reigns , it is impossible to conquer poverty
and shall Remain invincible. All revolutions in the name of
poverty were fraught;
The poverty was used by rulers as lever to perpetuate
themselves in power

Unless people themselves become master of their destiny,
humanity
Shall always remain subservient to the forces of vested interests
irrespective of
Ideology, types of governance under all; be it communism,
socialism

Socialistic republic or capitalist forms of governments. The genesis of the problem lies in mala fide intentions of the rulers. The day rulers use their authority as responsibility, a new era of hope will dawn till then, poverty shall remain the biggest enemy of humanity on earth.

By Mamutty chola

WITHERING RELATIONSHIPS

March towards goodness is always a
Journey through hurdle ridded routes
Like as if you are climbing a hill top
And fall from glory to infamy is like
Running down from hill top to bottom ground,

Alas! What a change in human values. The one
Whom he taught as child how to walk by holding
his hands, has now pushed him out of his house
In the twilight of his life .No respects for parents
who would sacrifice everything for
Their children's better future.

Lessons learned, never forget those faces
Who helped you when needed most
And never forget those who betrayed you
In whom you reposed your faith
Real friends/well-wishers are not those
Who come at your funeral but those who
Don't allow you to die while alive

Freedom with danger is better than
Be a liberated slave in your life .

Human tongue is the most powerful weapon
You can conquer the whole world without a
shot being fired, with love and care
Ironically, man is the only creature
who carries poison in his tongue.

Relationships are like gardening. There comes
A time weeding out of wild growths becomes
essential   for the health of the garden
So is life, there comes a stage when irrevocable
Differences take roots. In such eventuality it is
Better to part, then to live a life of compromised
without love and trust; the soul of human relationships.
By Mamutty chola

PROMISE OF TOGETHERNESS

Lived to experience that phase of life,
When my love's promise of life togetherness
Till death do us part was like writing on the sand.
she went away like floating clouds to land of
unknown; never to return

What to talk of human being, even birds migrate?
From withering trees and shift their nests to lush green trees.
Gone are the days of undying loyalty and togetherness.
Now everything is subject to change in life except self-interests!!

After a long gap came her letter when opened, it was blank
With few tears drops conveying her helplessness The reply
Which I wrote could not be posted as there was no address.

After gap of many years, I happened to glance at that letter
when opened the ink was still wet as if the words were mourning
in grief over the broken promise!!!
By Mamutty chola

Our Tomorrow Is Hidden In Today!!!

What is autumn and spring?
What is sadness and happiness?
What is death and life?
What is tear and smile?
What is defeat and victory?
What is failure and success ?
What is arrogance and courteous?
What is desert and greenery?
What is inaction and action?
What is hell and heaven?
What is intolerance and tolerance?
What is separation and union?
These are two aspects of our lives
Being human, it is next to impossible
To remain immune to the eventualities of life
One who understood this reality
Lived to lead a happy and joyful life
Oh man! live in today which is reality.
Has anyone seen tomorrow in one's life?
Trust me, our tomorrow is hidden in today!!!!
By Mamutty chola

MY NATIVE PLACE ANDAMAN AND NICOBAR ISLANDS

My native place Andamans is situated in Bay of Bengal
Away from Mainland connected by Air and ship from
Kolkata, Vizag and Chennai
It is a cradle of social harmony and peace
Alien to communal hatred, caste and creed and religion

It is the dream land of Gandhi, and Nehru
The cultural ethos unites all as true secular society

It is the land of freedom fighters from all parts
of undivided India. During 2nd world war many of our
ancestors were martyred by Japanese invaders including
my both grandfathers; maternal and paternal.

Though I have been away for years but still I remember
my schools, those big trees under its shades we would
play with friends during recess and our teachers who taught
us the values of human tolerance.

My native place is well known for its enchanting and
mesmerizing scenic beauty. Has already become one of the
famous tourist resorts in India
The mighty sea waves have always been my inspiration
In life to fight on. They have a big role in my struggles
from obscurity to Corporate visibility on mainland

The real ideal of India; unity in diversity can be felt and experienced in my native lace; Andaman and Nicobar Islands. Though I have been away since 1969 with intermittent visits, the values of tolerance, humanism and secular ethos are an integral part of my upbringing;
The real gift of my native place.
By Mamutty chola

Music Is Language Of Nature

Have you ever heard the music of earth?
Have not you seen green meadow dancing in bliss?
Have not you seen the flow of the river?
Have not seen the dancing branches of the trees?
Have not you seen the dancing waves in the sea?
Have not you seen dancing peacock and deer in the forest?
Have not you seen the birds in group flying amidst clouds?
Have not you seen the ice covered mountains like brides?
Have not you seen the young village girls singing on swings?
Have not you heard the early morning calls from mosque for faithful?
Have not you heard guruwani from the guruduwars in the early morning?
Have not you heard enthralling musical bells from temple and church?
Have not you heard raindrops falling on your rooftops and trees?
Have not you seen the greenery all around after first rain?
Have not you seen leaves falling in autumn and advent of spring?
Have not you seen young children playing and dancing on first rain?
Have not you realised the music is omnipresent in all nature's creation?
Have you ever realised all divine scriptures are composed in poetry?
Be it Quran, Gita, Bible, Torah, and gurugrath saheb so music is within us.
Therefore, our earth is the best musical orchestra in the universe. LET US PROTECT IT.
By Mamutty chola

MIRROR'S SUBMISSION

I know my limitation
Not in position to teach
My humble efforts are
To make all realise
The importance of retrospection
Never feel sad after looking at your ugly reflection
Never blame me for your ugly look
I, as a mirror, exist to tell the truth
I being a mirror not aware of world's diplomacy
I am at loss why people are scared of my existence
My existence is truth and nothing but truth!!!
My only quality is that even after broken, retains my originality.
By Mamutty chola

CIRCUMSTANCES REASONS FOR WORRIES

*Strange is human nature; tolerate criticism
But get angry over the silence of others*

*The man of culture knows the importance of
Feelings and concerns; signs of civilized man*

*What a human tragedy we all spend time pleasing all
Results; loved ones never satisfied, the satisfied were not yours*

*It is wrong to presume; difficulties are reasons for
Adverse circumstances. The reverses is the truth*

*Remember all human relationships rest on
Trust and mutual respect for each other's*

*Whoever understood these realities
Always lived to enjoy happy relations*

*Failures and setbacks are good teachers
To err is human in the best tradition of Adam!!*

*If someone repeats a point of view with swearing
Trust me he is lying; never trust such person in life.
By Mamutty chola*

TIME IS INVICIBLE

Nothing is more kind and cruel than time
Friend to friend, enemy to enemy
One quality of time which is unmatched
Whether happiness or sadness does not last
Whoever kept pace with time always a success
Whosoever did't respect time disappeared into oblivion
Have a glance at history, whoever kept pace prosper
All achievers down the ages are products of time
Time give equal opportunity to one and all; be a king or a pauper
Though time is invisible but remains with us all the time
Time is power, time is wealth, time is happiness and fame
Time is omnipotent, omniscience and omnipresence
So magic of time is matchless and infinite.
By Mamutty chola

TRIBUTE TO FATHER OF THE NATION

*Q*uote Intolerance is itself a form of violence and an obstacle to the growth of a true democratic spirit.Mahatma Gandhi Unquote

M K Gandhi, our father of the nation was an incarnation of noble soul representing human excellence.
A true Hindu with extreme tolerance for other religions; essence of Indian ethos, values and centuries old civilization His determination was mightier than the mightiest then empire on earth. Through sheer power of moral courage , he brought the mightiest empire of earth on its knees and got freedom for India from centuries old colonial rule.
He always believed that greatness of humanity not being human but humane !!He believed in the invincible power of love even for his killer.
He had earned a place in people's heart across the world , He was an inspiration for Martin Luther king Jr and Nelson Mandela in their fight against oppressed regimes .
If we, as a nation had followed his path; India of today would have been different country; free from hared, violence, greed and power. There is an urgent need to learn and practice his values in our daily live politicians and rulers in particular and public in general to usher in an era of prosperity, peace and tolerance in our midst, the best homage.
By Mamutty chola

MY LOVE, MY PARTNER IN LIFE

I am indeed grateful to Almighty for the gift of ever loving companion
In life. She is matchless in her love care and dedication like dream realised.
She left her loved ones for me since there were religious divine between us.
Love being secular and above prejudices she chose me over her family decided to spend rest her life as my companion in life. She has been the inspiration for me to fight on in life. She being beside I could rise from obscurity to corporate visibility in my long journey in life. But for her love and care it would have been next to impossible. Indeed it has been power of invincibility of love.
Despite passage of years of togetherness, our love for each other has grown leaps and bound
From strength strength. Her ever charming smile gives me inspiration to love life never before. Her beauty, charm, grace and her long flowing hairs like dark majestic clouds take me to land of bliss.

We still visit sea shore as we would do our college days playing with sea waves. An eternal
Inspiration to humanity to fight on and never give up. Our very sight make the waves to dance and touch our feet expressing their abiding love for us .
I wonder at times this life would have been incomplete without my love being part of my existence

Her beauty still reminds me of dancing peacock , song of nightingale, dancing deer in the wood, and birds flying in the sky amidst floating clouds

Her eyes are like serene lake, her lips are like rose petals, her face like blossomed lotus. Her smiles takes me to the land of bliss amidst meadows, dressed with greenery in spring

Even the nature is in love with my love; be it birds, wind, rain all sing in praise of her beauty. Our love for each other is immortal..Our relations are inseparable in every life till eternity.Our love being rooted in soul is immortal, our love will remain ever young and ageless be in this life and next life.

By Mamuttychola

FRIENDS AND FOES

If all are happy with you in life
Definitely you have tolerated others shortcomings

If you are happy with all in life
Certainly you must have ignored other mistakes in life

When you are successful in life
All be; it loved ones, friends or strangers will hold you high esteem in life

When you are down in life
You would come to know who are your real friends   in life

Never trust people who are opportunists in life
Trust always trustworthy and dependable in life

Never aspire and regret for things beyond your reach in life
 Be focused on things which are achievable in life

If you want to realize how rich you are in life
Think of those possession yours which money can't buy in life

The beauty can be a reason for happiness in life
But the happiness has always been the reason for beauty in life

I am not creature of circumstances in life
I am the creator of my own destiny in life.
By Mamutty chola

SAGA OF MOTER'S GLORY

As a child and as a student I have had heard and read many
Stories about saga of mother's glory.
First; because of sacrifice. Love and devotion, Quran says
Paradise is at mother's feet.
Second example; there was mother despite poverty and hardship
brought her son up and given him the best education in life.
But when married, he became a henpacked husband
His wife had a pathological dislike towards his mother.
She forced him to shift to a separate house leaving old mother to
Fend for herself in her old age. Not only this one day she told
Her husband if he really loved her , then go and kill his mother
And bring her heart. Just to please his wicked wife, he did kill his
 mother and while running and carrying his mother heart
He fell on the ground, there came a cry from his mother heart
asking her son, did you get hurt my son, take care!!!
Third example goes back to Napoleon era. Among many British
Solders he had captured, one was found escaping and swimming
Across British channel in a stormy weather. When caught and
brought before Napoleon and questioned the British prisoner
said
When he had started for war, his mother was very sick, he was
concerned about her wellbeing and wanted be with her.
Napoleon was pleased with answer, he ordered the prisoner be
released
And told the prisoner he salute his mother and pay his regards
Being mother of such a brave son,

Fourth example was bad influence of mother's upbringing. There was a boy who would steal and his mother would encourage. When he grew up he became professional criminal and committed many murders eventually caught and sentenced to be hanged. When asked his last wish, he expressed his desire to meet his mother. At gallows under the pretext of embracing he bit his mother ear, she cried out in pain. When questioned, he said if his mother had cautioned him not steal when he was child, he would not have become criminal!!

The mother being the best gardener, her role is matchless and unparalleled, indeed.

By mamutty chola

TRUE LOVE IS IMMORTAL

The one whom you try to forget
But still Lives within you, It is
called true love.

The one who's very thought inspires
You to excel in life, it is called true love.

The one to whom by losing you feel victor
 It is called true love.

The one whose anger makes you love her
It is called true love.

The one about whom you keep thinking
It is called true love.

The one who left you like gone time
But you still wait for her thinking she
would come back like season
It is called true love.

You often would tell her love always demands
sacrifice when you were together unmindful of
Destiny's cruel designs.

Love being rooted in soul, love is immortal
Because soul is immortal too.!!
By Mamutty chola

Success Is A Transit Camp

Excellence is not a destination
It is a never ending journey

A journey of infinite
Will remain on till eternity

All achievements are always transient
For time and circumstances change

Past milestones are guides
History is events of dead past but left
A mark on time canvass for posterity

Never follow known paths
Always follow untrodden path
In pursuit of new frontiers

In human civilization
All high ways took birth
From the womb of footpath

So is the case with all cities
All emerged from the womb
Of slums and hutments

Before construction destruction comes
Human civilization is nothing but saga of destruction
Constructions, events, struggles, victories
Defeats, joy, sorrow, celebration and mourning's.

By Mamutty chola

www.ingramcontent.com/pod-product-compliance
Lightning Source LLC
Chambersburg PA
CBHW031311160426
43196CB00007B/491